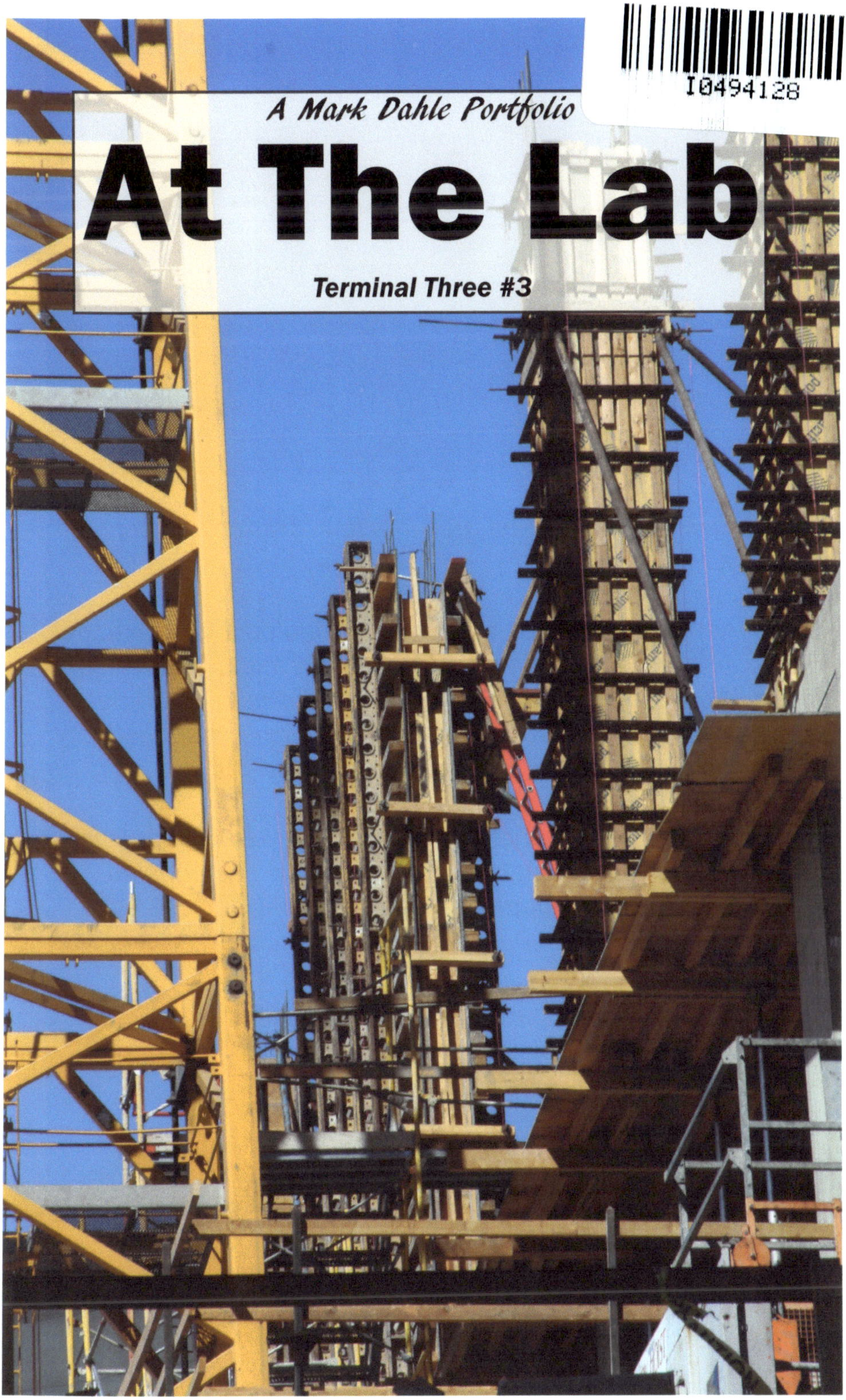

A Mark Dahle Portfolio

At The Lab

Terminal Three #3

Mark Dahle Portfolios can be read in a few minutes and enjoyed for a lifetime.

Unlike many picture books, the text is not related to the beautiful painting at the right and the photographs that follow. This might seem a little weird at first. One thing that helps is to order more portfolios until you get used to it. In the meantime, feel free to draw your own pictures of Cooper and the lab if you like.

This portfolio includes a photo of a brilliant 36 x 24 inch painting (at the right), twenty-seven beautiful pictures of Los Angeles, California, and a story about members of the resistance checking out a lab that supplied them with vaccines.

Photographs in this book are available in very limited editions. See http://www.MarkDahle.com for more information and for previews of upcoming portfolios.

We do our best to create portfolios free of editing mistakes. But it's hard to catch everything. We reward people who report errors in any Mark Dahle portfolio. For details see MarkDahle.com/Typos.html or email MarkDahle@aol.com with the subject line "Typos." Thanks!

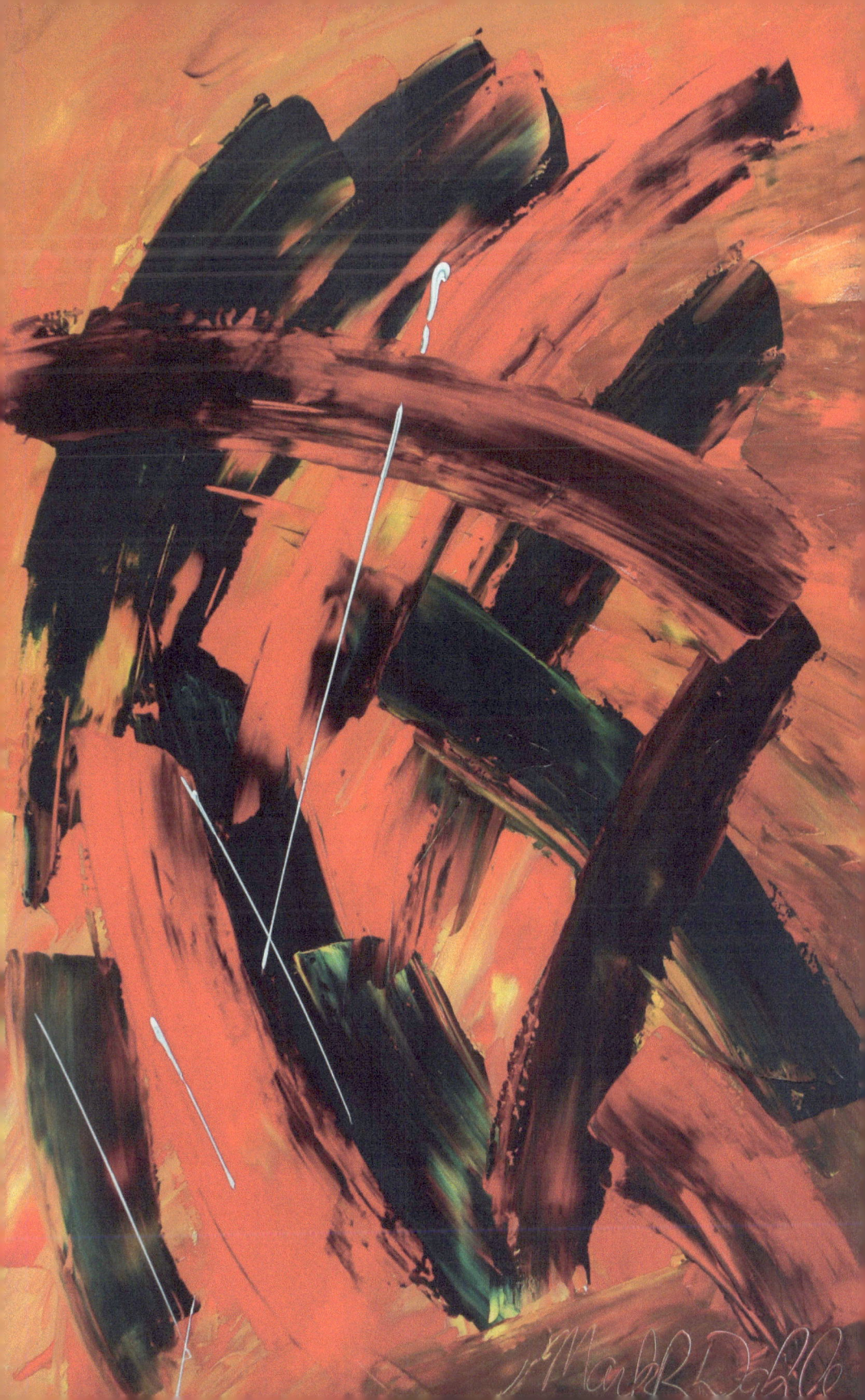

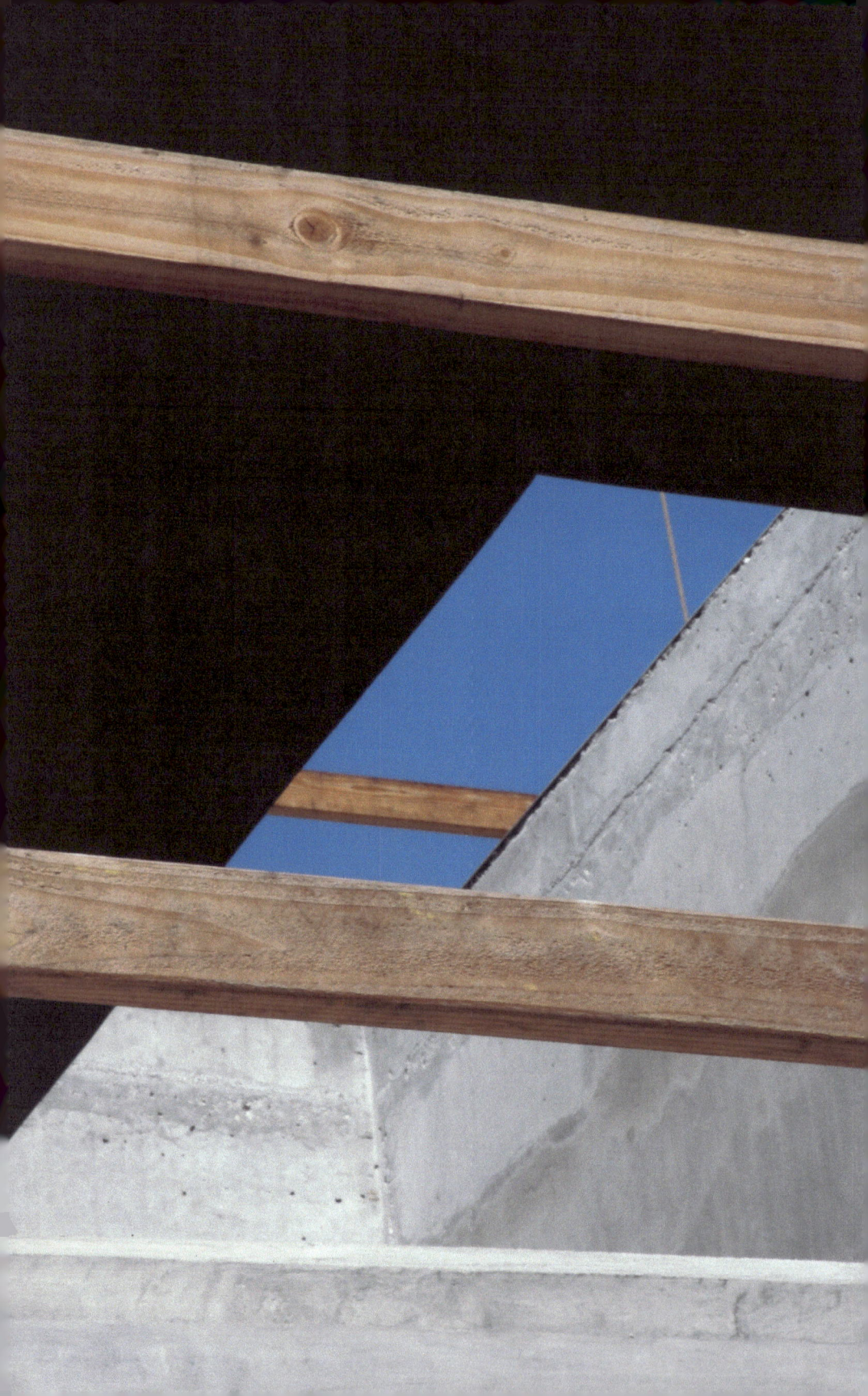

Cooper missed his NewsGraph implant, but he (and the rest of the underground team) had access to information from the feed at many sites hidden throughout the city. At those sites they could also connect with the underground's smaller databank. Cooper was heading to such a location now.

He wanted to check out a troubling question Han had posed: were the makers of the MalPox vaccine still alive?

Rather than head straight to the lab, Cooper decided to first learn what he could about his contact.

The NewsGraph reported the standard bio he would have expected, with nothing unusual. It was only when he queried the underground databank that he discovered a curious bit of data.

The face of the researcher who had been his contact for the MalPox vaccine matched that of an actor who had appeared in two minor film productions. It wasn't the normal track for someone whose life was consumed with research. Cooper decided to visit the researcher's house before going to the lab.

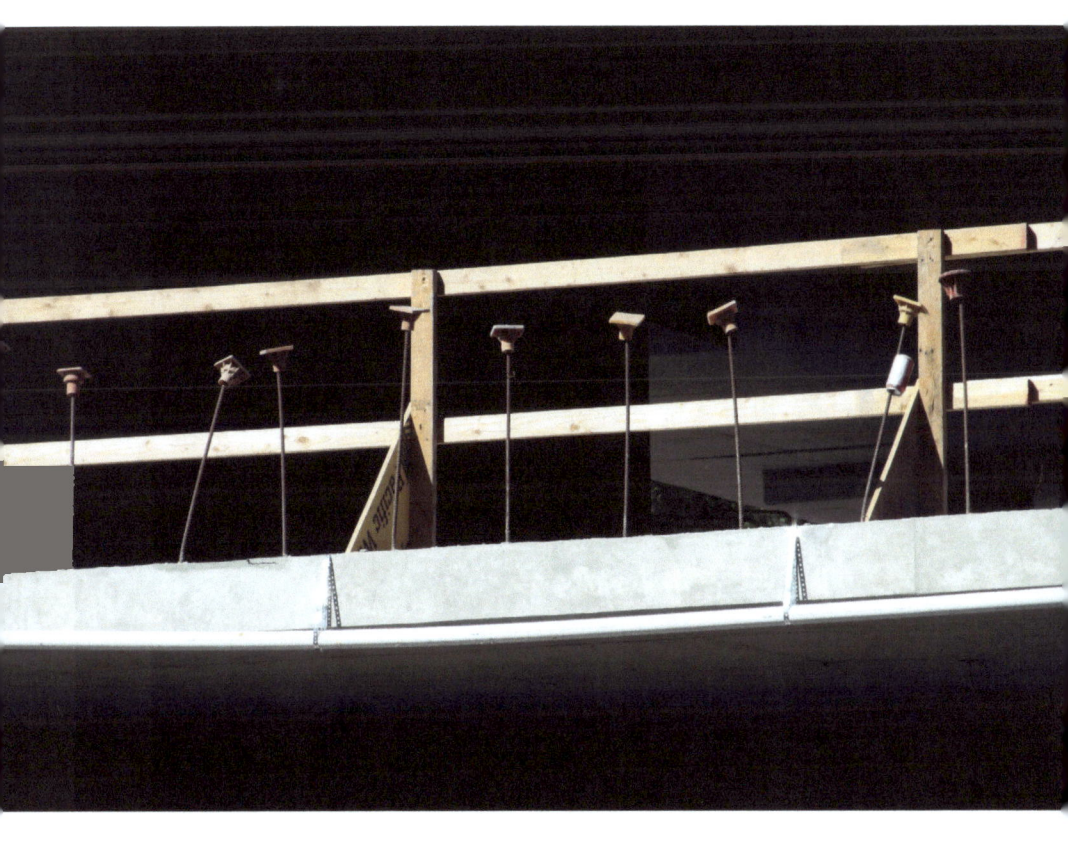

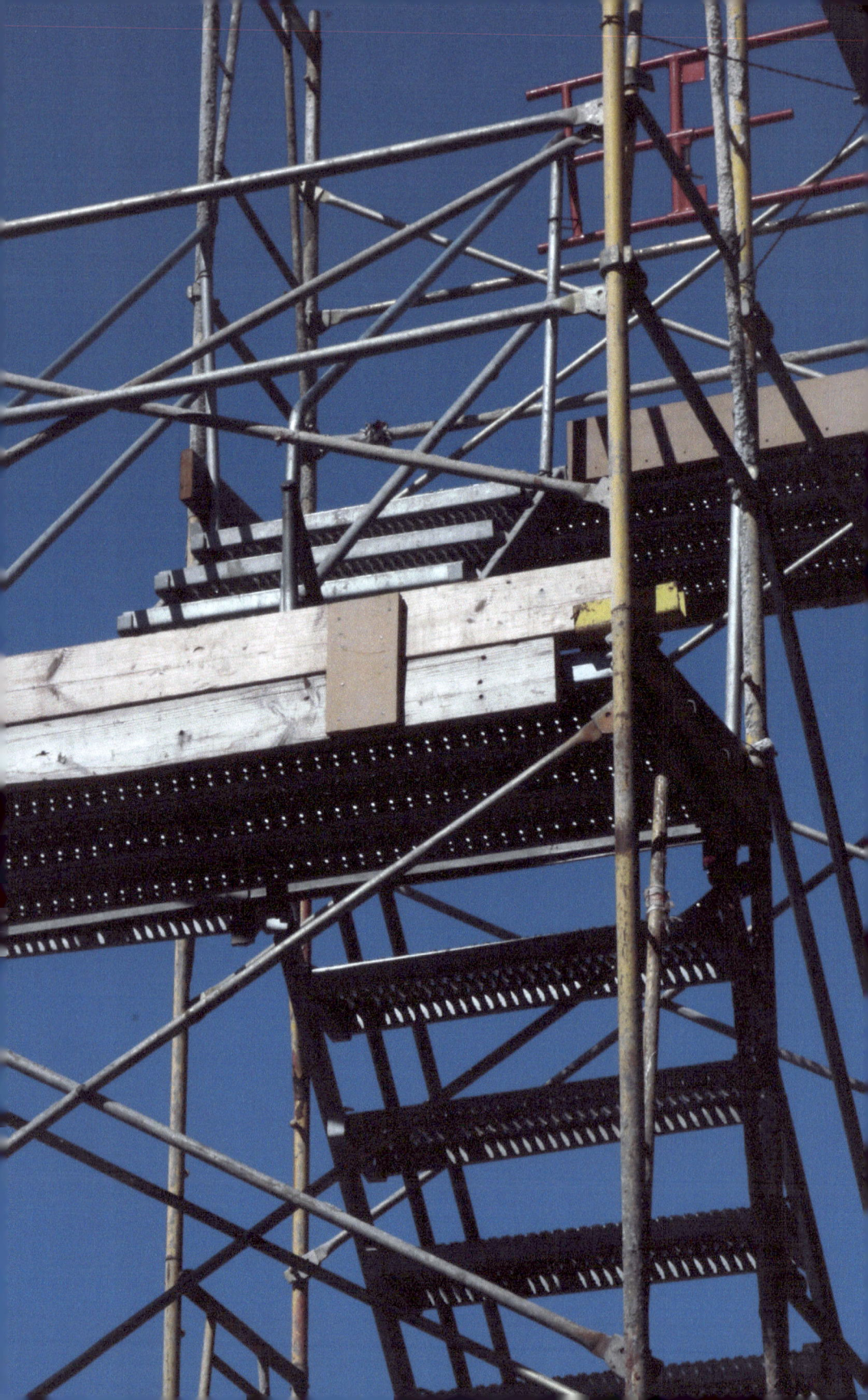

When Cooper arrived at the modest home an hour later, no one answered the front door. Cooper walked around to the back. Before he could knock, a young woman emerged from a neighboring house holding a Stunner.

"Who are you, and why are you here?" she demanded.

"I'm Jess Parks," Cooper said, using the alias the researcher would know. "I came to see Tom."

"You have the wrong house. Now beat it before I call the SecurPatrol."

"Tom Fischer doesn't live here?"

"Oh!" she said, her voice changing, her eyes squinting briefly. "Mister Fischer. Why didn't you say so? What do you want with him?"

"I'm Jess Parks," Cooper repeated. "I need to discuss some research he was doing for me."

"Stay there and do *not* move. I have something for you. I'll be right back."

She retreated to her house and emerged with a package and large envelope.

The package had "Tom Fischer" written on the outside. The envelope was unmarked.

"You can have these on three conditions," she said, still aiming the Stunner at his head.

"I'm listening."

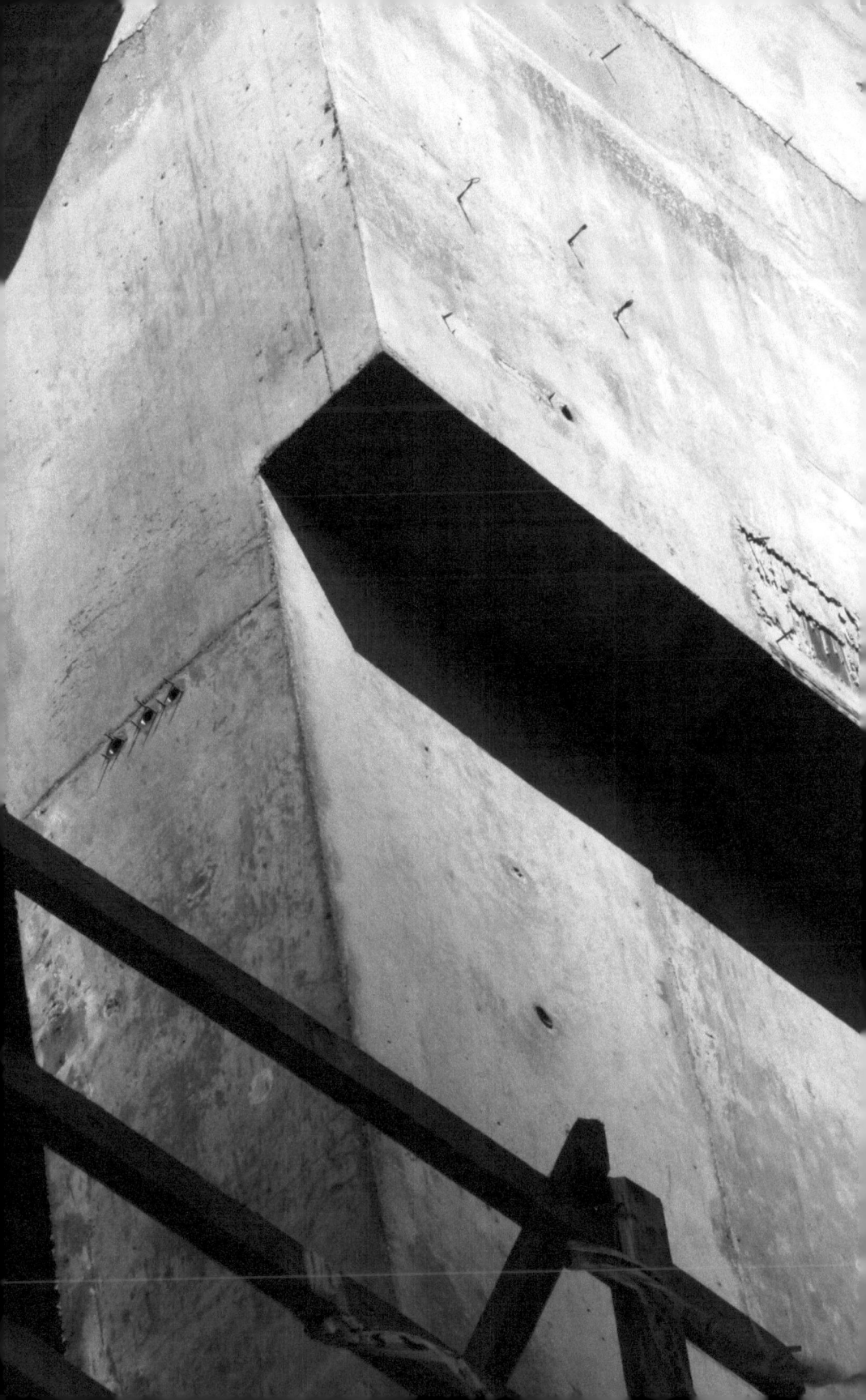

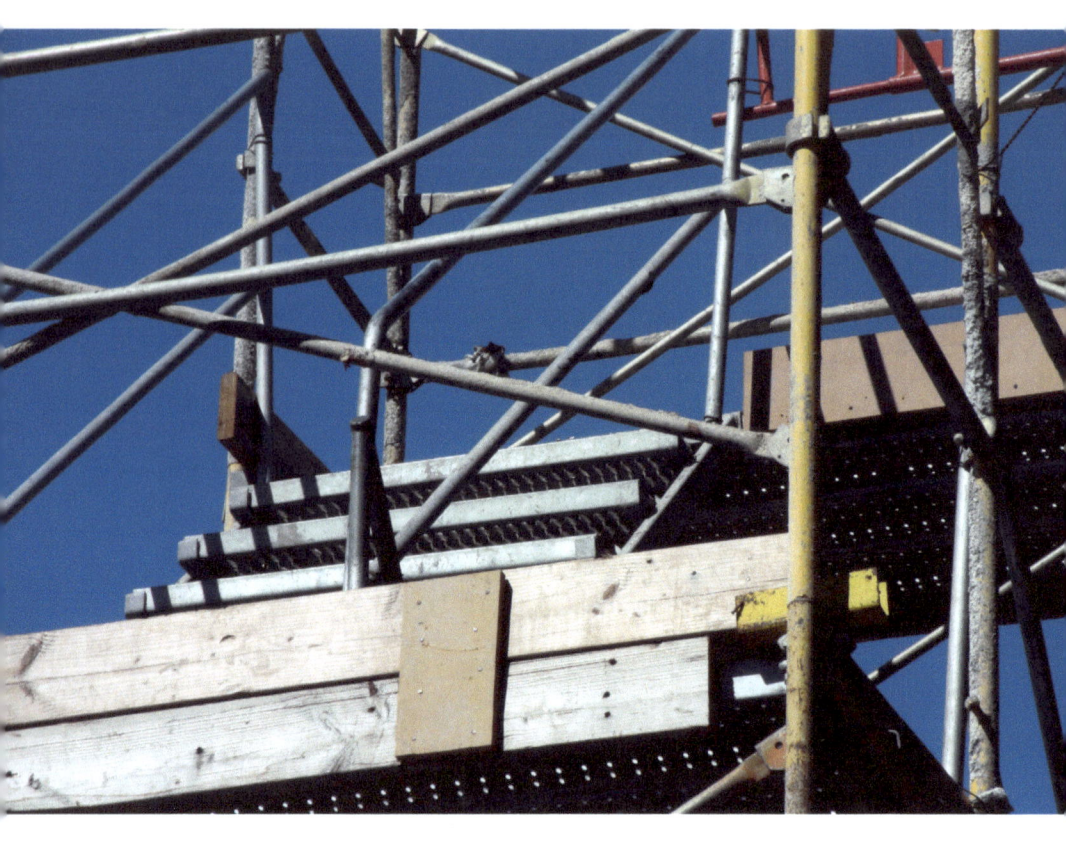

"You're not to open either one until you get to a secure place."

"Easy enough."

"Second, you're not to come back here. I've been waiting for you for a month and I'm leaving as soon as you leave. Jack's – I mean Tom's – family cleared out three weeks ago. They left no forwarding address."

"And the third condition?" asked Cooper.

"Hold still a moment," she commanded. She consulted her NewsGraph to see what hits came up for his image, but none did.

"Let me put it this way," she said. "Neither Tom nor I know if we can trust you. We're both taking a chance giving you these. But if I ever find out that you're *not* a friend of Mr. Fischer, I *will* find you. And I'll bring something besides my Stunner."

Cooper thought about replying, but he had nothing to say that might help.

He *wasn't* a friend of Tom's, just a client, and until he saw what was in the packet, he didn't know which side he was on.

So he just nodded.

Shelly set the envelope and package on the ground, then backed toward her house, keeping the Stunner aimed at his head.

"Take the packages and go," she said when she got to her door.

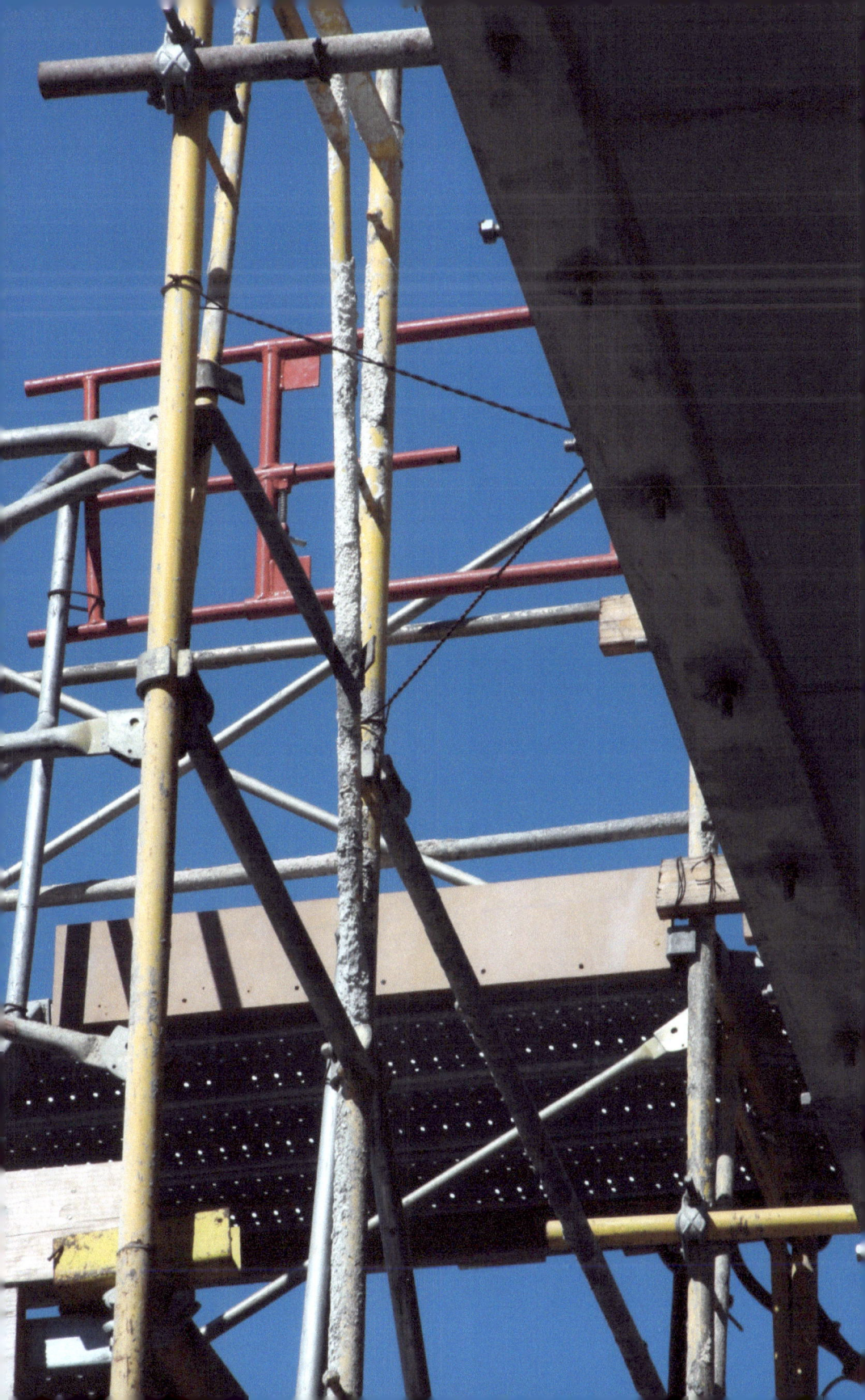

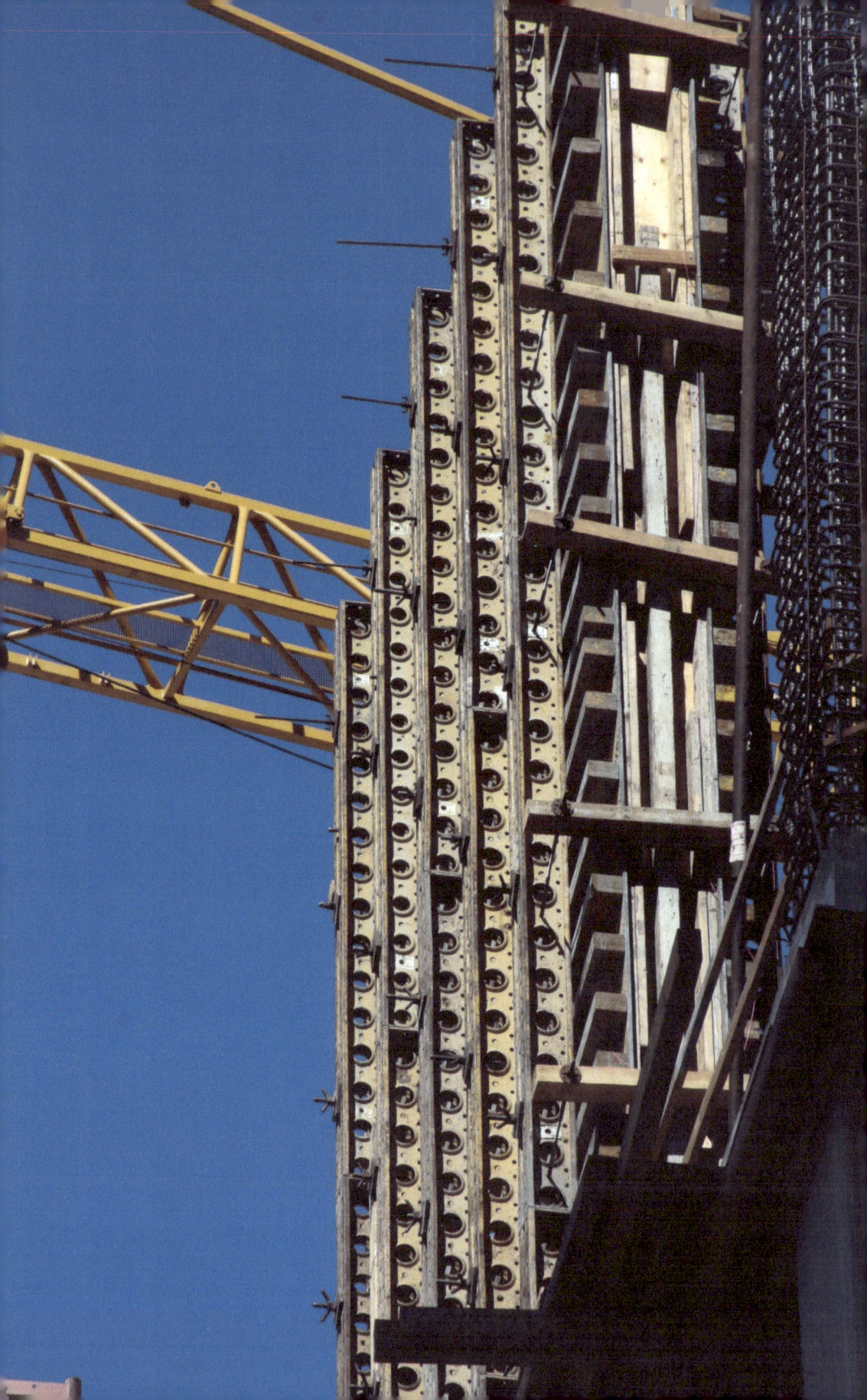

As soon as Cooper left the neighborhood, he used a SecurSweep to check the package and envelope. Neither contained a tracking device, not even NanoBots.

He had no way to check for MalPox or other biohazards, but at least his location wouldn't be traced if he carried the package to an underground site.

When Cooper was finally back in a secure environment, he opened the envelope. It contained a funeral notice for Jack Barnes, an actor who had a few minor roles before his sudden death at age 42. Jack's picture was an exact match for Tom Fischer. Jack had died six days after Cooper had asked the lab to create the MalPox vaccines.

The larger packet contained a copy of two films Jack had appeared in and a VidNote. Cooper ignored the films and started the note. Tom's face appeared.

> My name is Jack Barnes. I'm an actor. I was hired this week to play Tom Fischer, a lab researcher. We've filmed four days so far. Tomorrow is the last day.
>
> For four days I've read lines off a Teleprompter. The first two days all the lines were typical for a lab rep. "I'm sorry your order is delayed," that kind of thing. But on and on, eight hours a day. You can cover quite few situations in eight hours.
>
> Yesterday it was just individual words, phrases and sounds, I guess so they can splice sentences together if they have to, if they forgot to script something.

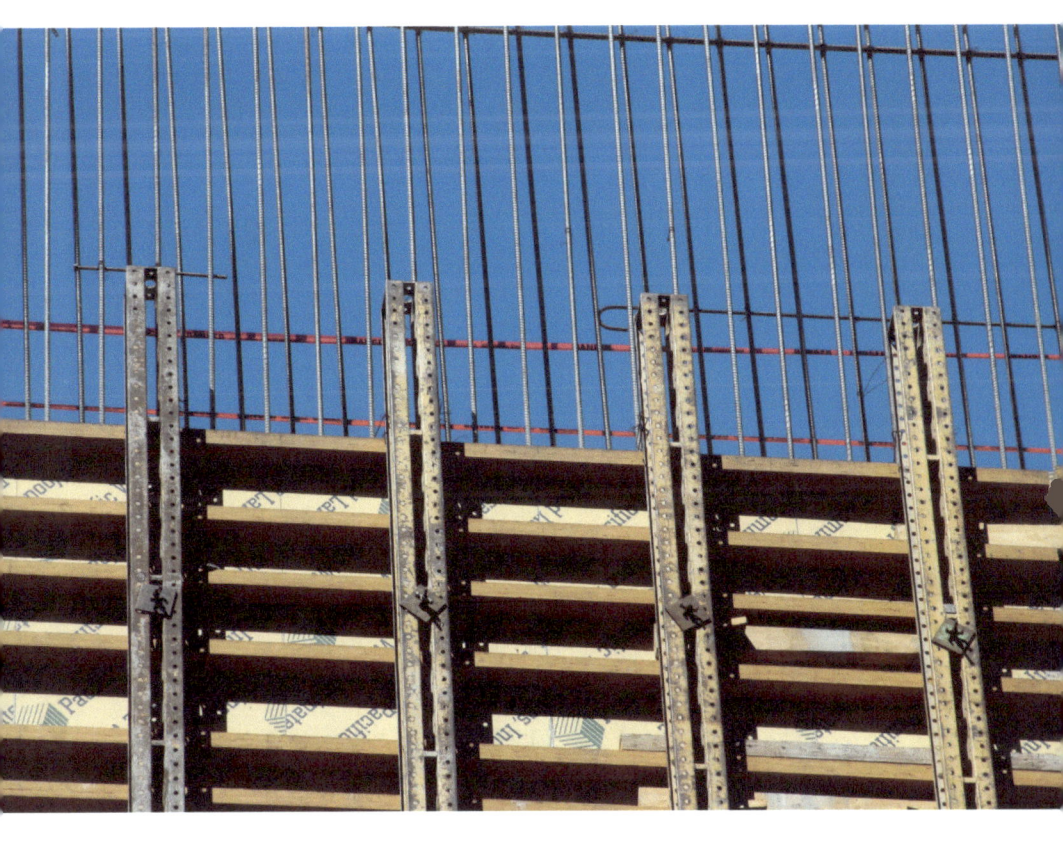

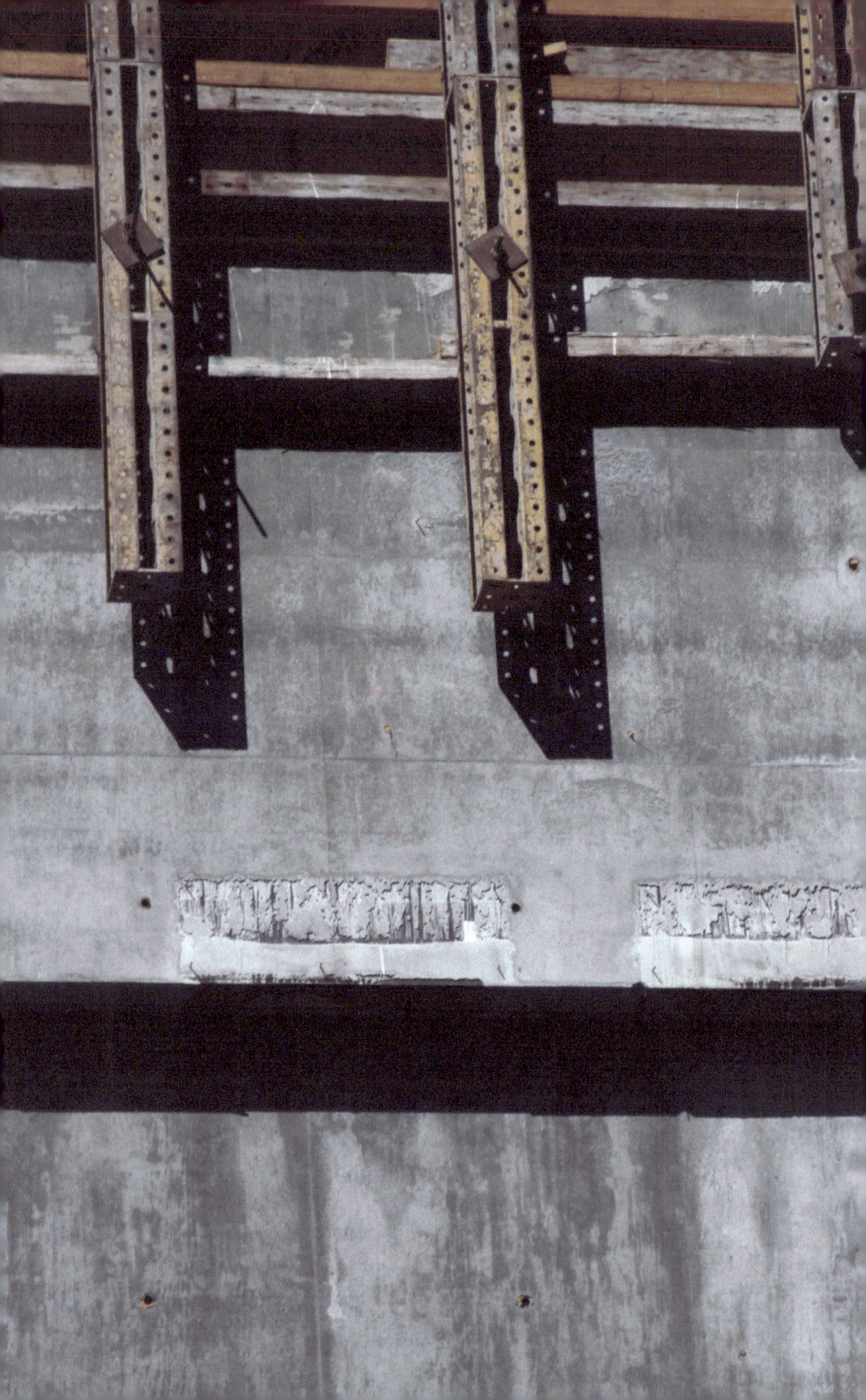

I'm guessing they're creating an autobot using my image. It's not a great acting gig, but it'll pay some bills.

But I'm recording this note because the situation has never felt right.

I haven't met one person on the set in four days – not a director, not a producer, not a stage manager or lighting director. Nobody. I show up and the camera's rolling. No makeup, nothing. It's not a normal set.

Hopefully I'm just paranoid. But just in case something happens to me, my neighbor has instructions to give this package to the first person who comes looking for Tom Fisher. Hopefully you're on the right team.

The main reason I'm so on edge about this project is that today all the lines I read were about catastrophes – all kinds of plagues and disasters and biohazards that wipe out life – and why the lab is not at fault. Not the kind of thing you expect from an autobot. And it makes me wonder if the lab *is* at fault, or will be soon.

The names I've read have included every region I can think of, anywhere, from Saturn to Earth.

Hopefully I'm just working on a creepy movie with a weird director. But I made this note just in case.

The note was dated the day before Jack died.

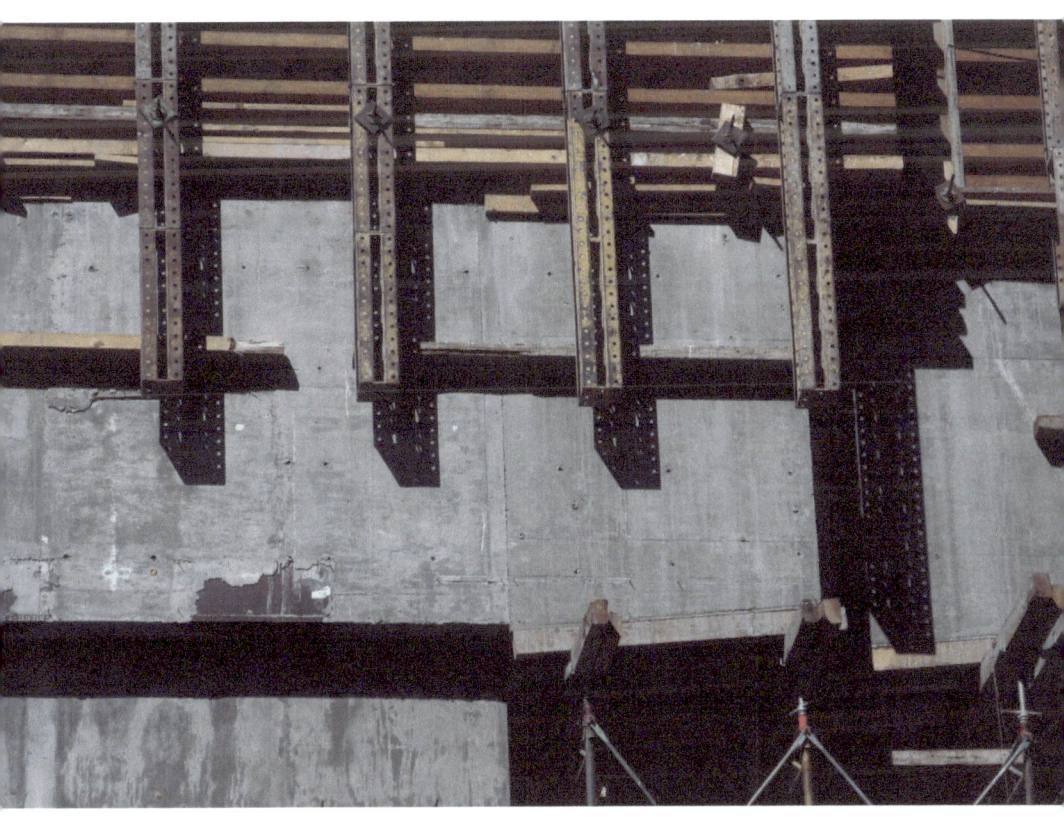

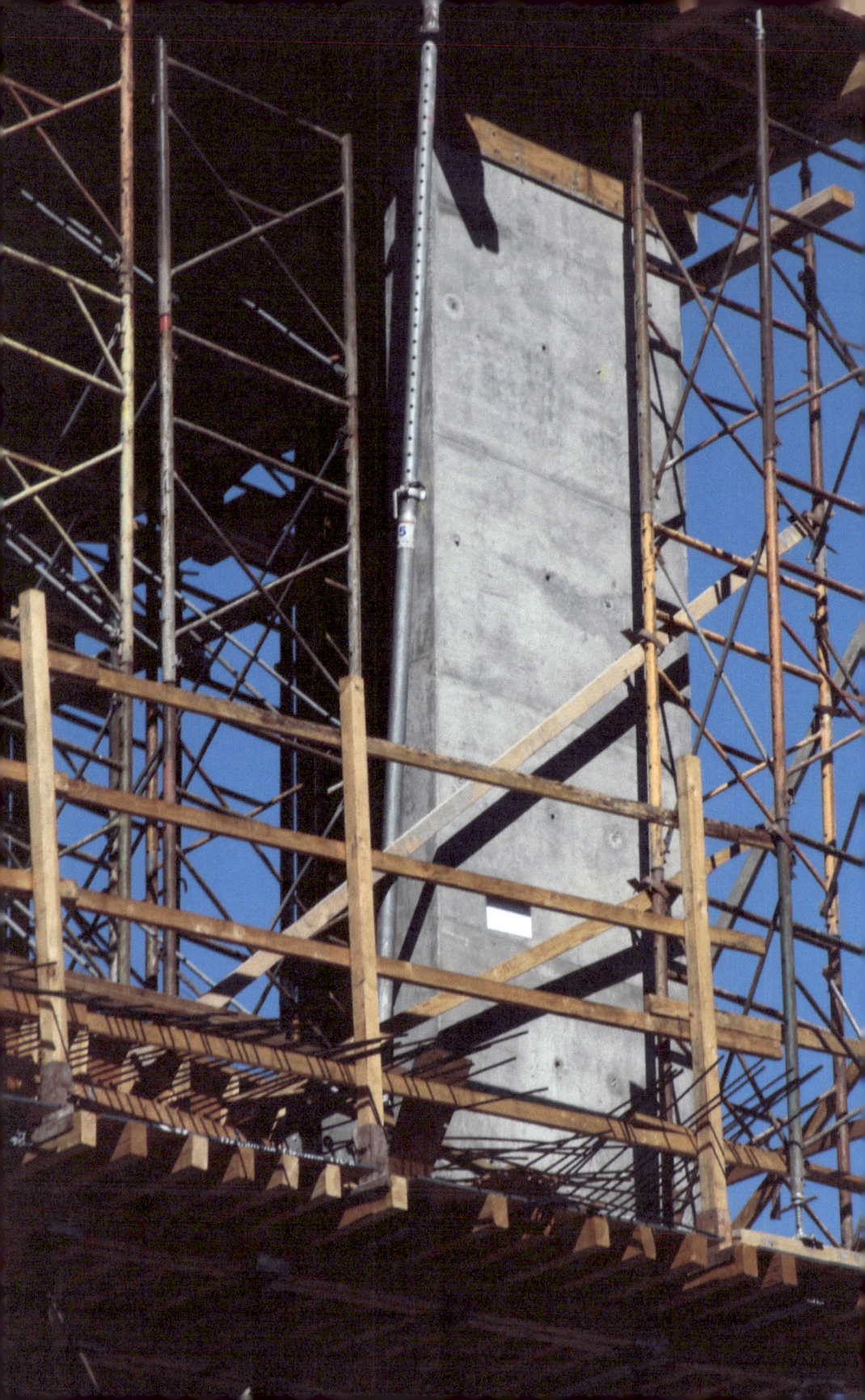

When Cooper had first contacted the lab by text, the lab had scheduled a video conference for the following week.

A quick check of the dates confirmed Cooper's suspicions: when Cooper met Tom via video, Tom was already dead.

Cooper debated going to the address of the lab after seeing the VidNote. But he decided to risk it, to see what was there.

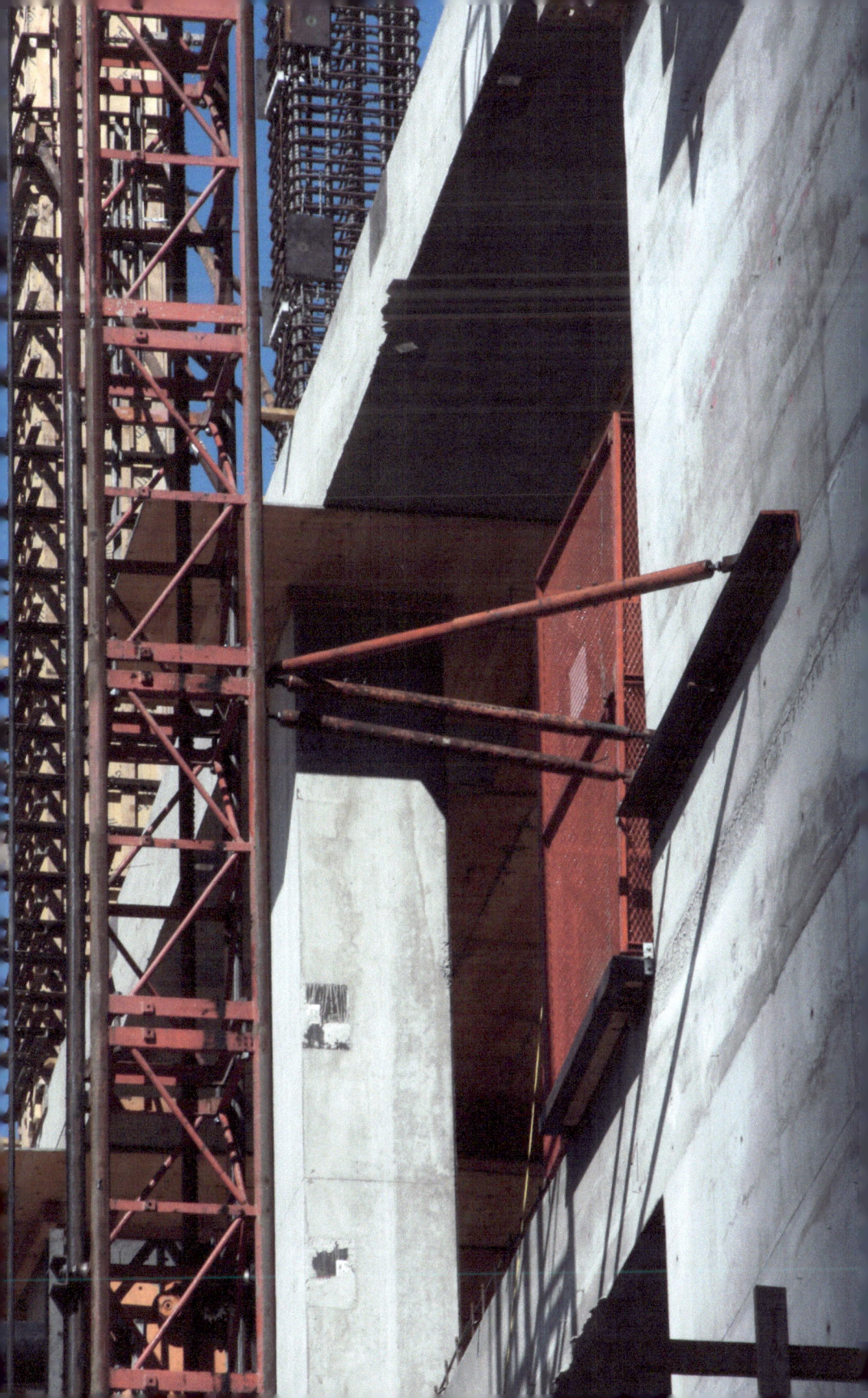

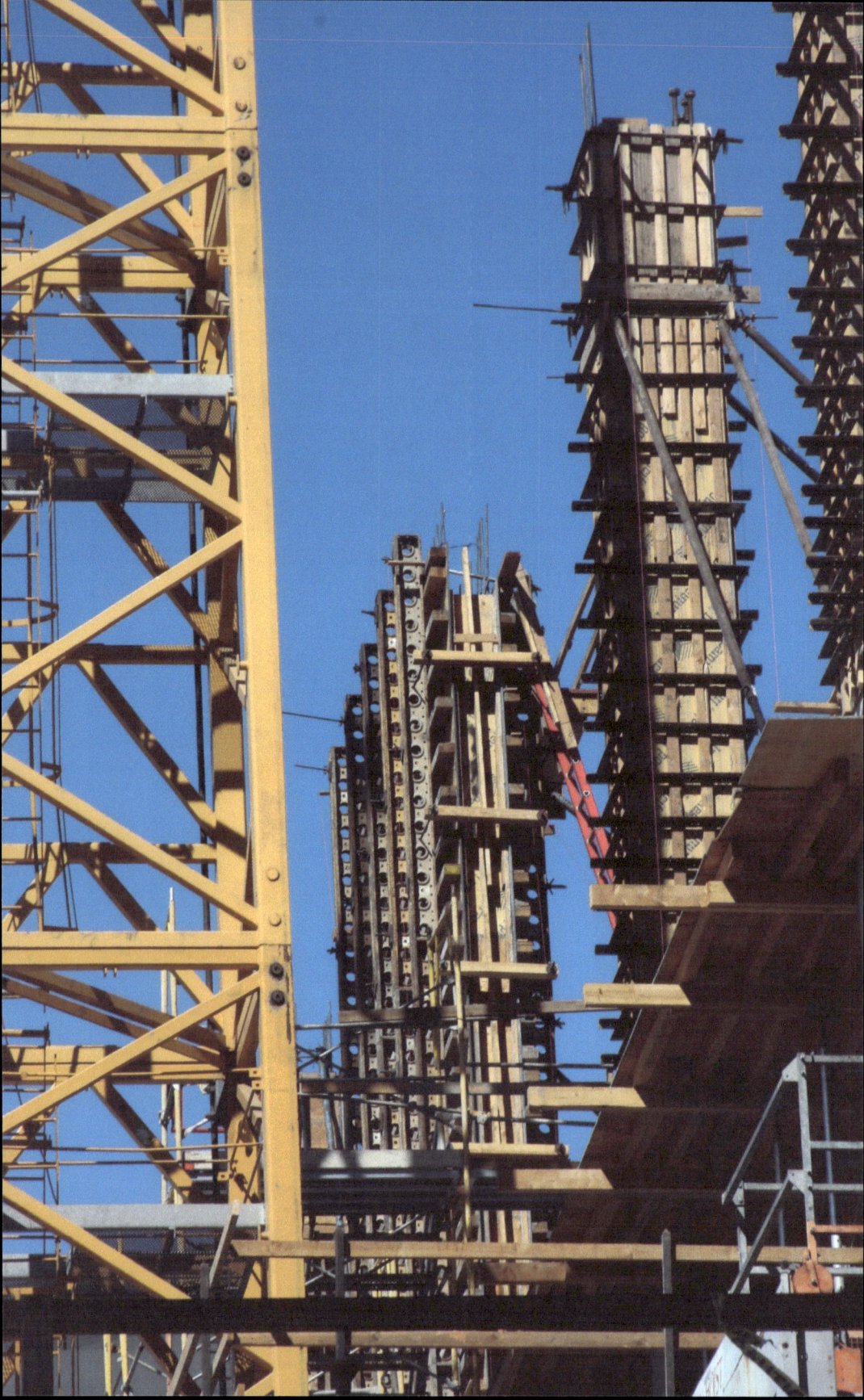

The lab was hidden away in a corporate park, with no sign on the door. Cooper let himself in.

The reception area held a few chairs and a table. As he entered, a video screen lit up and Tom's image appeared.

"Hi Jess!" Tom said. "I've been wondering how your tests have gone. I've been watching for news from the quadrants and I haven't noticed anything."

"Right," said Cooper. "That's why I'm here. There was some glitch in the test – we're not sure what happened. We haven't heard anything either. We've decided to run the test again. I'd like to get another dozen doses, four of each of the three strains. Any chance you could prepare them for us this week?"

"We'll get right on it. It shouldn't take more than a few days."

"Alright. Call me when they're ready."

"You bet. Anything else?"

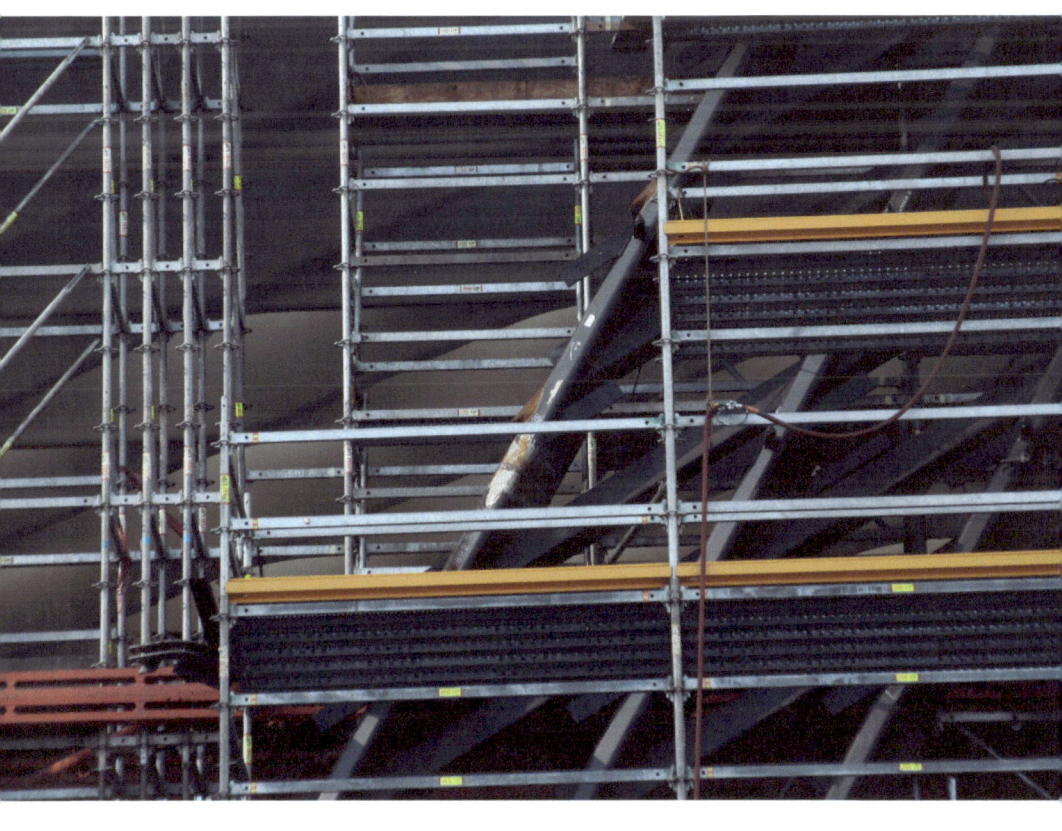

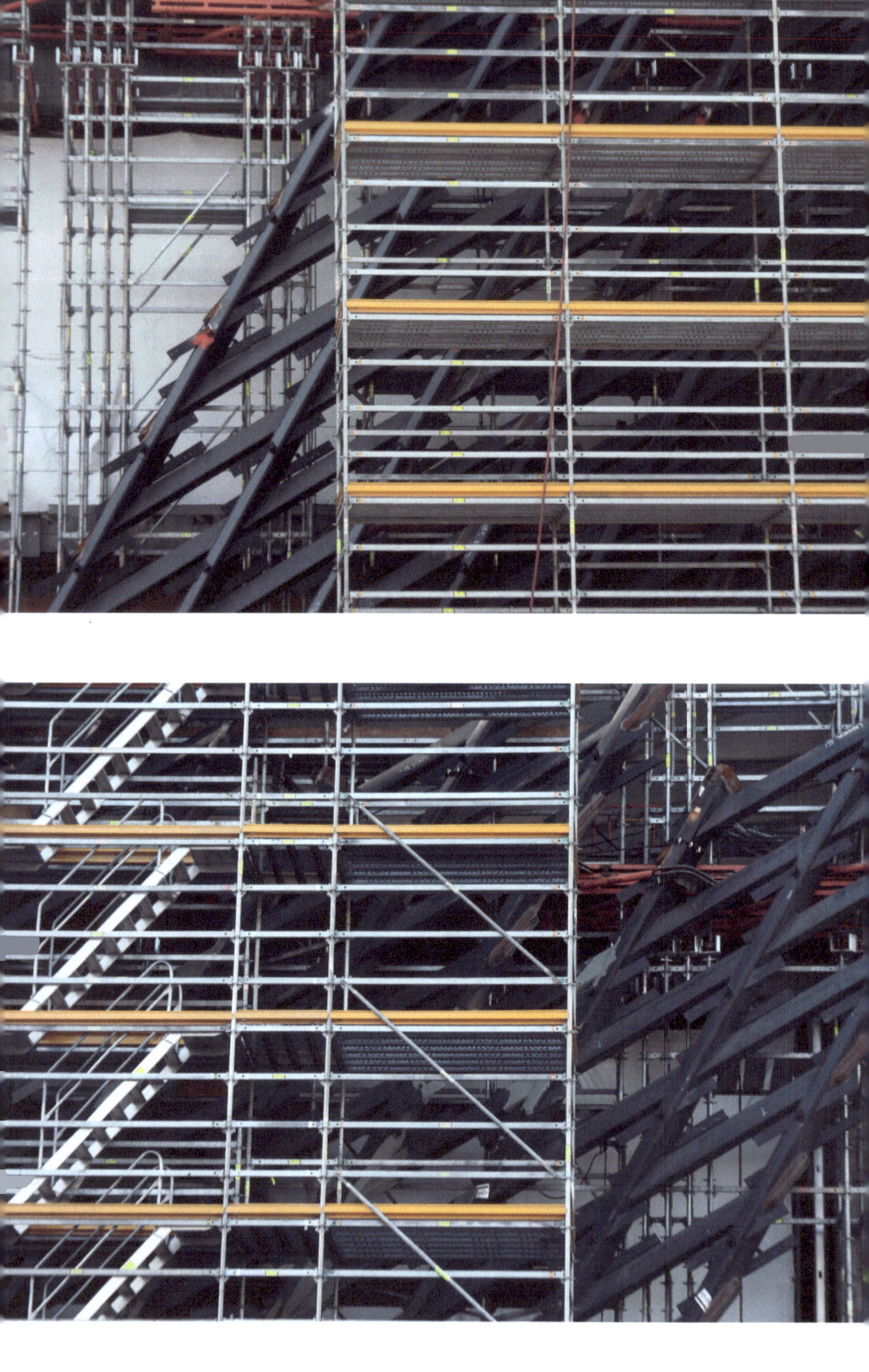

"No, that's it," said Cooper. "Thanks."

Then, as if an afterthought, he said, "Oh – well, yes. There is one more thing, just for fun. I'd love to get a tour of the lab sometime."

"Hmm," said Tom. "Normally that's not allowed – both for security and to maintain a clean environment. Plus the lab is not that interesting, since everything we work on is so small. But I'll check and, if we can't do a tour, I'll at least send you a video of our operation."

"Thanks," said Cooper.

Cooper left, knowing the whole conversation had probably been recorded and that his face, heart rate and perspiration levels would be analyzed for signs of dishonesty. He had eliminated the tells from his face and heart rate a long, long time ago. But facial measurement was getting so sophisticated he had no idea what might have been detected.

Three weeks before, when placing the original order, Cooper had appreciated that his conversations with Tom were by VidLink. Video conferences were convenient for people in the resistance. It was safer than travel.

But now he realized, having seen the site in person, the real lab might be anywhere in the world. The reception area might be all there was at that location, just a small room overseen by a dead actor and whatever controlled the video feed.

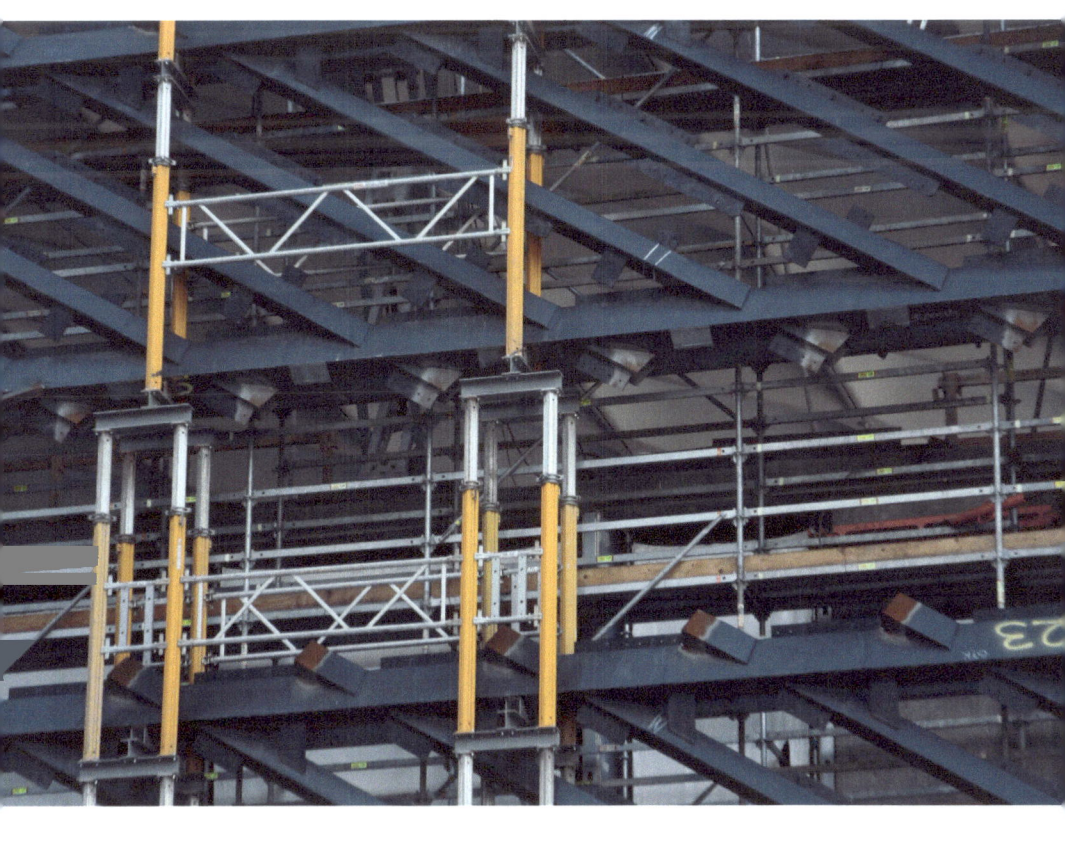

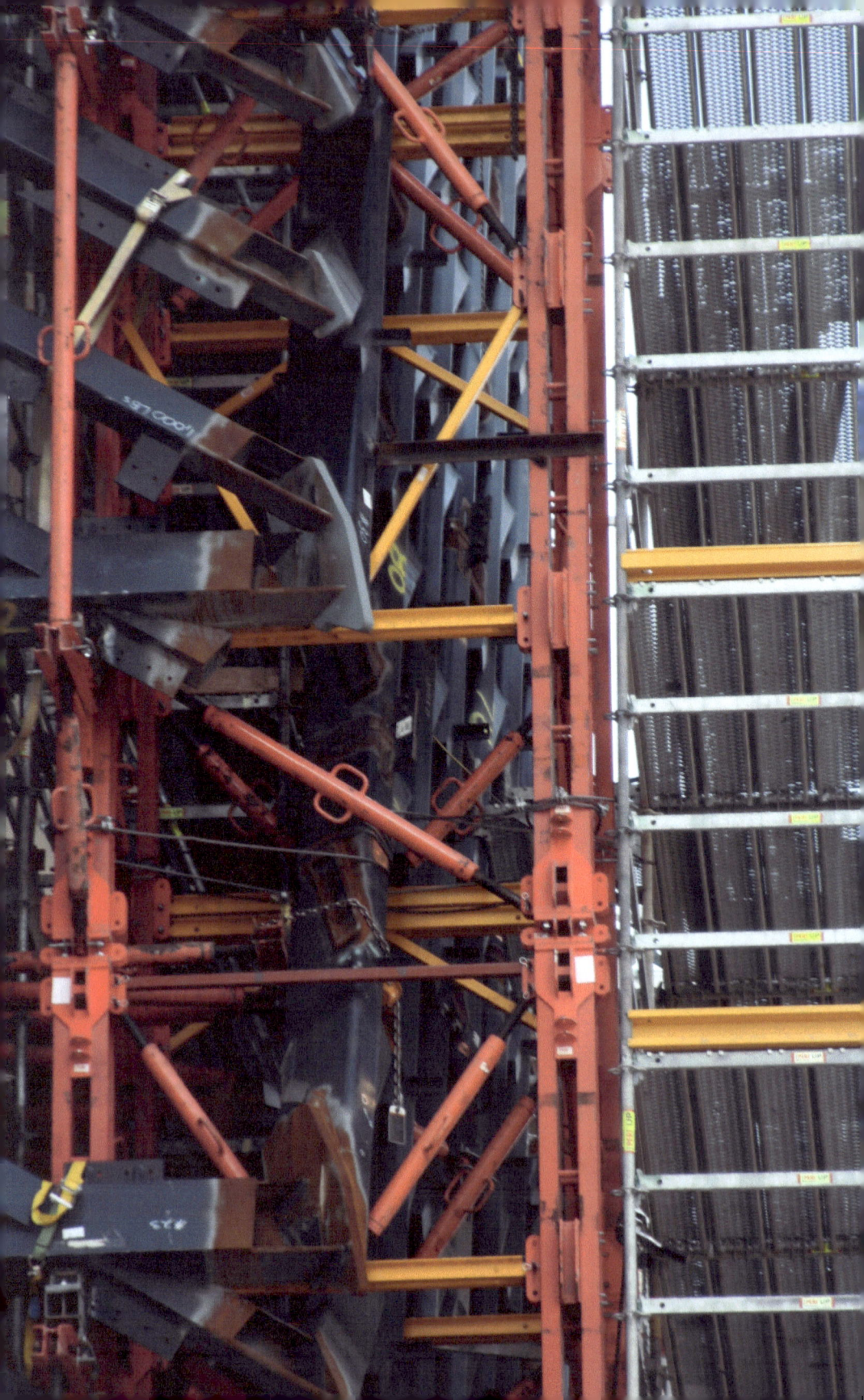

Cooper didn't have time to watch the films Jack had sent, and Han needed something to do that didn't involve much movement. So Cooper briefed Han and gave him the task of trying to find out why Jack had sent the films.

The first film Han watched wasn't great, and Han felt his attention wandering. Why *were* the movies included in the package? Was it really just to show that Jack had been an actor? A clipping would have sufficed. Or a quick glance at a NewsGraph. Did Jack just want to be remembered if something happened to him? Or was there something else? If Jack had another reason for including the movies, what would it be?

Han drummed his fingers on the bed. His experience with the Braazoid had made him cautious. He copied the movie file before starting to examine the code.

It took Han several hours to piece it together. He had been working with the assumption that there would be only one encrypted message, and instead there were two, both scrambled and running on the same track as the video. About three a.m. Han finally figured out how to split the image into thirds. When he did, he pushed the call button on the wall.

When Jana looked into his room, she found images on three of the walls – a B-grade movie on one wall and Jack staring into the camera and talking on the other two.

"If Cooper's asleep, wake him up," Han said. "He needs to watch this."

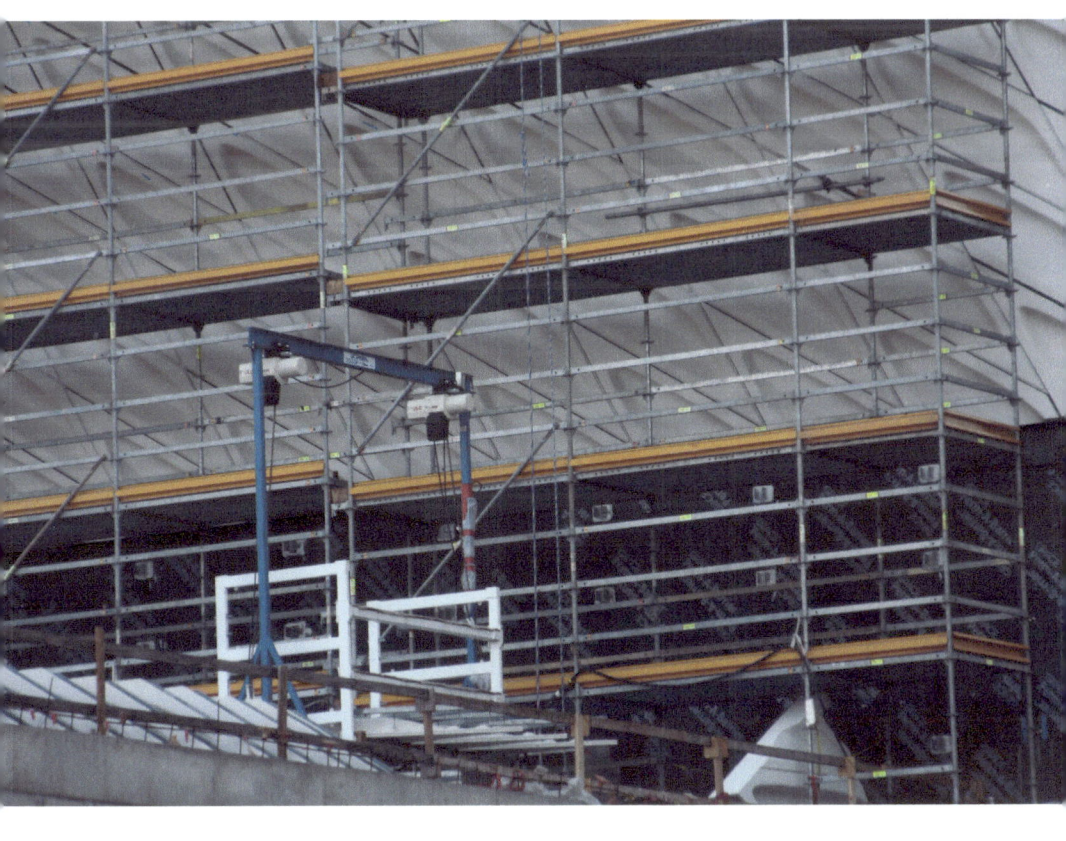

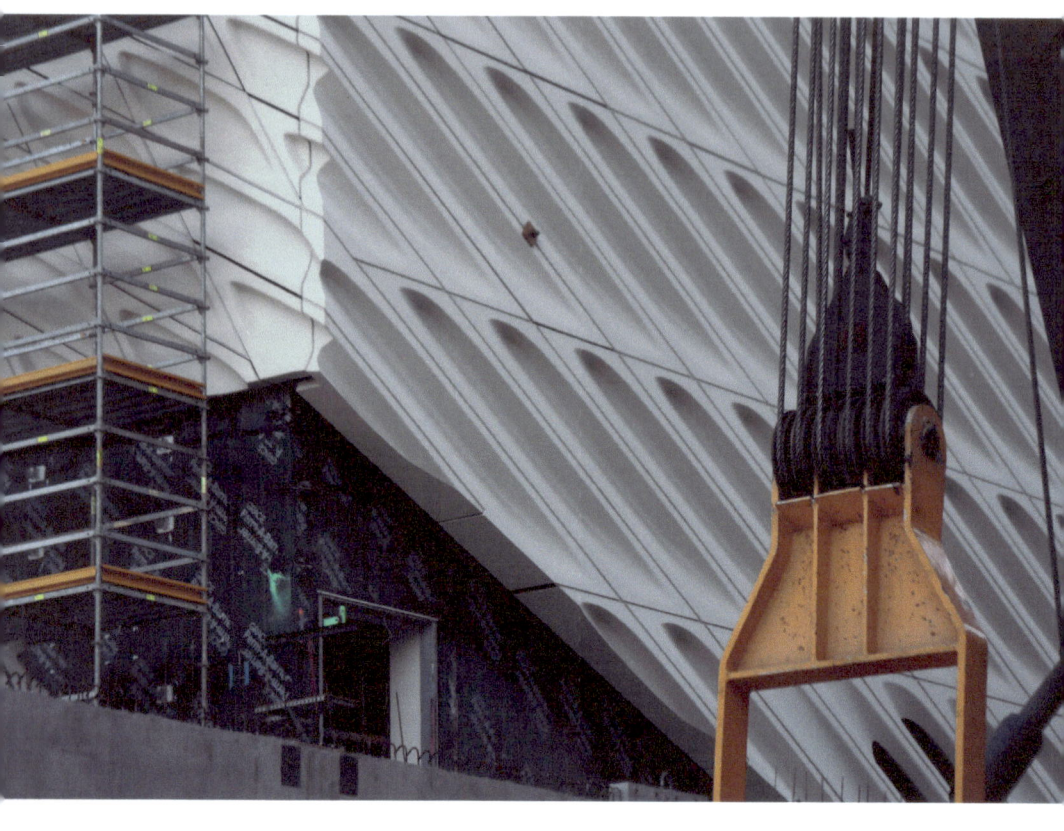

Jana returned with Cooper soon after. Han told them he had found nothing of interest in the movie so far, except as a delivery mechanism for the other two messages. Then Han switched the sound to the image on the second wall.

Jack was reading off the names of places.

Moon Quadrant A
Moon Quadrant C
Whitehorse
Lima
Mexico City
Tokyo 4
Tokyo 6
Kyoto
Pyongyang
Los Angeles West
Los Angeles at Phoenix
Venus Six
Jerusalem/Dubai
Santori Ten
Sao Tome
Chicago Minnesota
Singapore
New Delhi
South Sudan
West Palestine In Exile
East Palestine In Exile
Shanghai
New Moscow
The Plains
Rocky West
Duluth
New York/Washington
Baltimore
Saturn Sector 4
Saturn Sector C
Saturn Sector F

Han finally turned the sound down.

"These are the names of every place the flights went to when I was at Terminal Three. But the list doesn't end there. It eventually includes every city I've ever heard of."

In the background, Jack continued reading.
> Berkistan
> Venus Two
> Rome
> Paris/Madrid
> Beijing
> Rocky South
> Texico.

"I admit it's an odd list for a manufacturing lab," said Cooper. "But by itself it's not that incriminating."

"Right," said Han. "It's just a list. But check out the third wall."

Han switched the sound to that image.

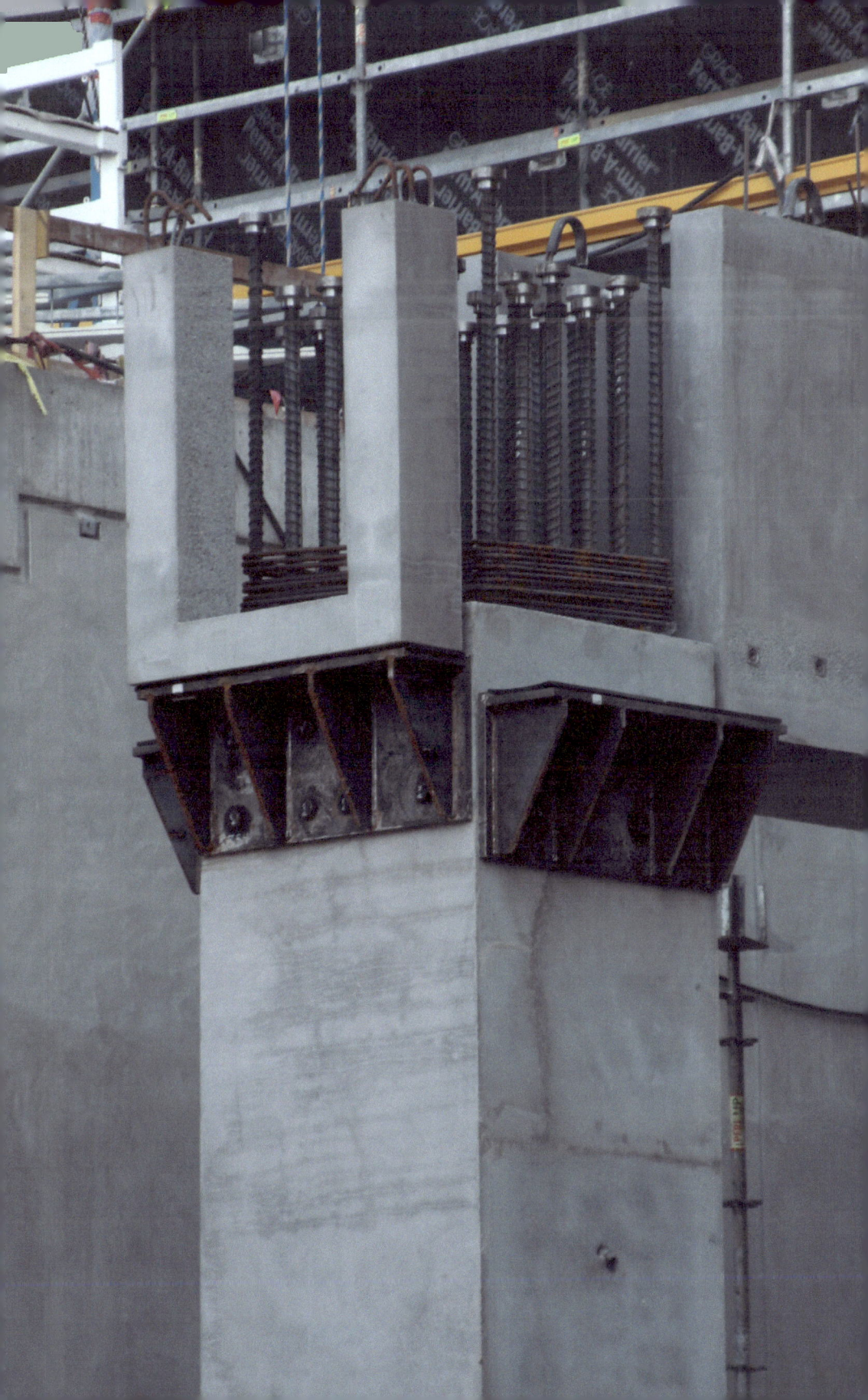

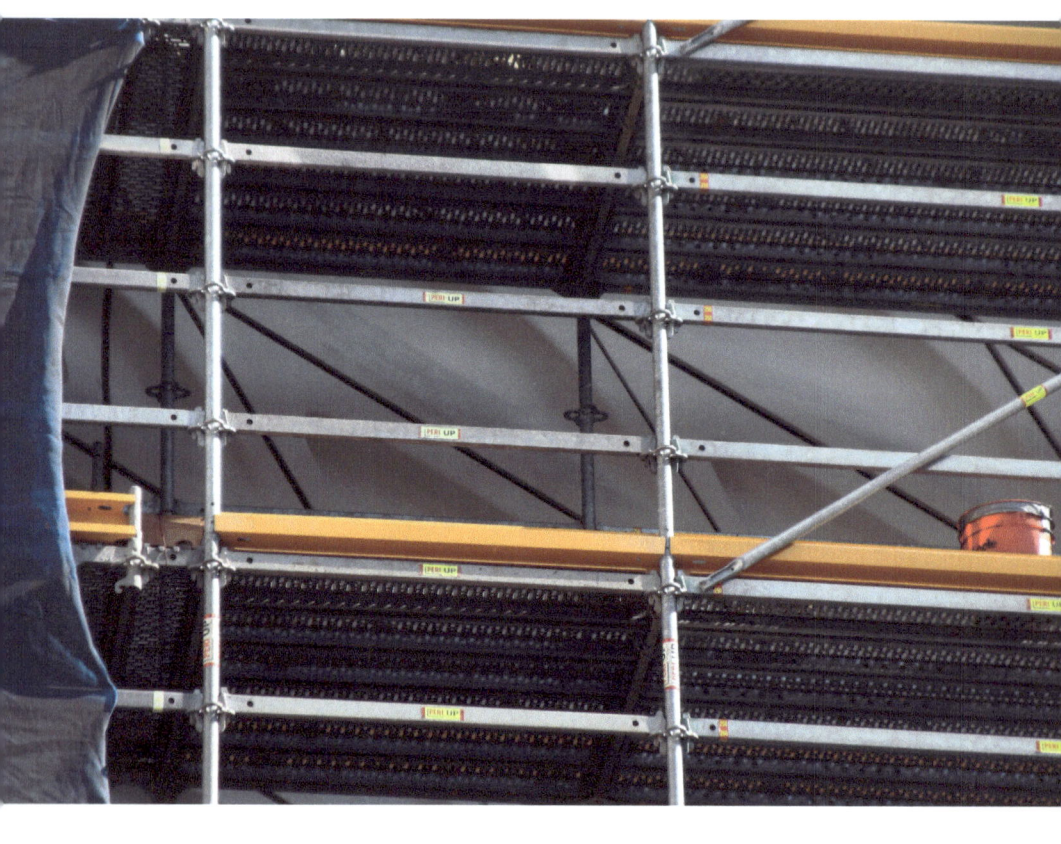

Jack was calmly explaining that the lab was not at fault.

> I don't know how that could have happened.
> There's no way our vaccines are involved.
>
> That can't be true.
> The vaccines are safe.
>
> The vaccines are not contagious.
> The reports must not be correct.
>
> The number of deaths in Whitehorse must be exaggerated. Besides that, there's no way the outbreak in Whitehorse could be connected to our vaccine.
>
> The number of deaths in New York/Washington must be exaggerated. Besides that, there's no way the outbreak in New York/Washington could be connected to our vaccine.
>
> The number of deaths on Saturn Six must be exaggerated. Besides that, there's no way the outbreak on Saturn Six could be connected to our vaccine.
>
> The number of deaths in Los Angeles West must be exaggerated. Besides that, there's no way the outbreak in Los Angeles West could be connected to our vaccine.
>
> The number of deaths in South Sudan must be exaggerated. Besides that, there's no way. . . .

The list of cities with outbreaks was endless.

No wonder Jack had been unnerved after the fourth day of taping. And if the information Jack had smuggled out was any indication, it looked like the deaths in Whitehorse were just the beginning.

"Okay," said Cooper. "Is there anything else?"

"That's as far as I've gotten," Han said. "I thought you should see this much."

"We've probably seen enough," said Cooper. "What do you think based on what we've seen?"

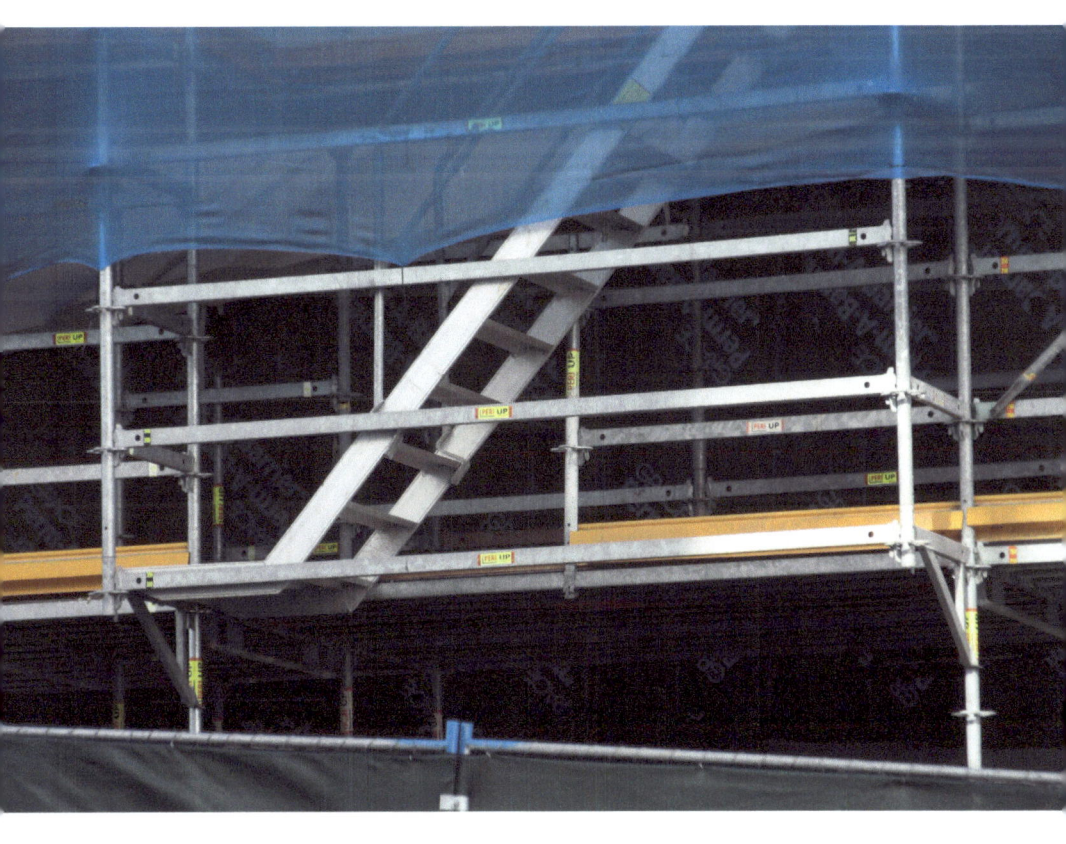

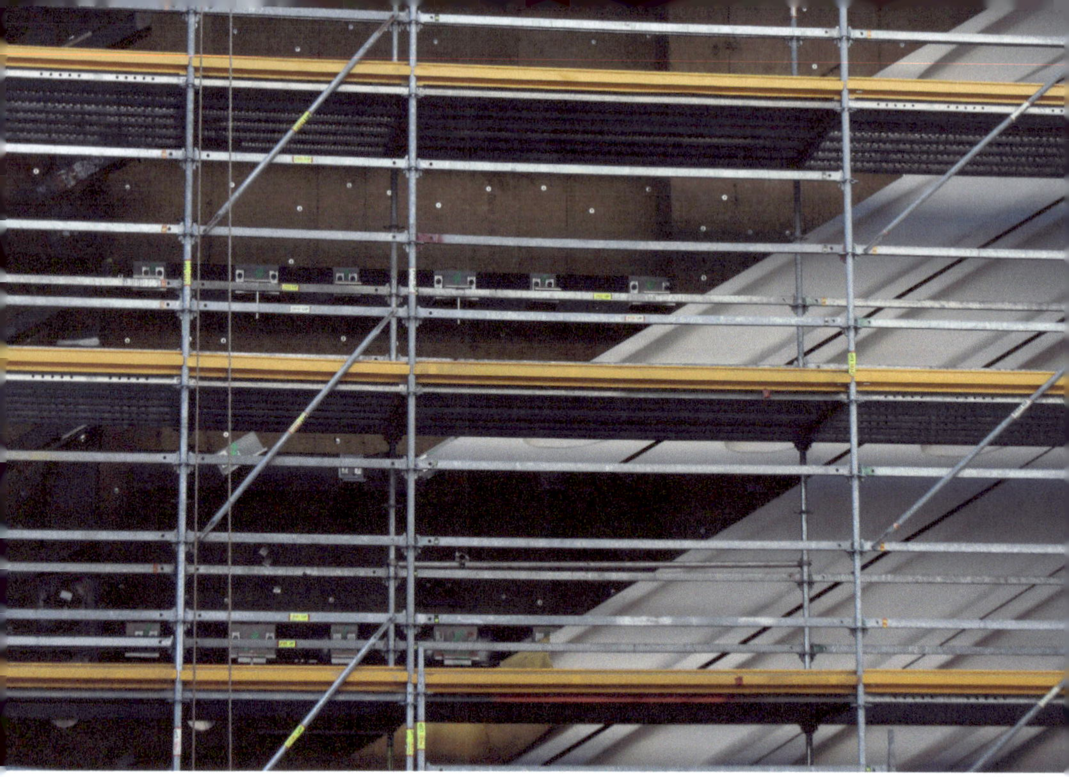

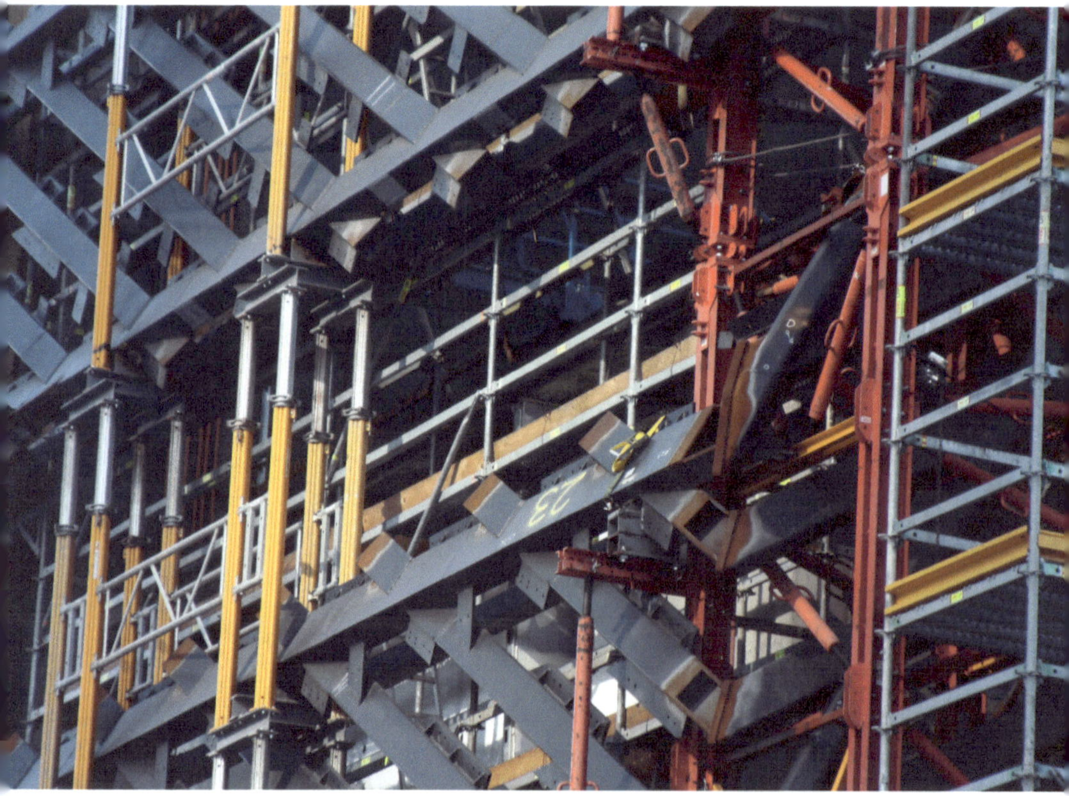

"Well," said Jana, "we know that what happened at Whitehorse wasn't an accident. Somehow they knew our volunteers wouldn't get to the moon and that there would be large-scale deaths."

"Right," said Han. "The *best* case with this last video is that, at the time they made it, they didn't know where the volunteers would be sent, so they didn't know where the deaths would take place. Or maybe they wanted to hide the real target in a long list. If they only wanted one target – the President and a good portion of the Otto Party – they wouldn't want Whitehorse to stand out, so maybe they buried it in a mountain of data.

"But that's only the best case scenario," he said. "Worst case, Whitehorse is just the beginning, and they expect MalPox to spread everywhere."

"Right," said Jana. "If they were trying to hide the real target of Whitehorse in a long list, that's good. Because otherwise it's like they don't care *where* the fatalities happen. It's like they want them everywhere."

~~

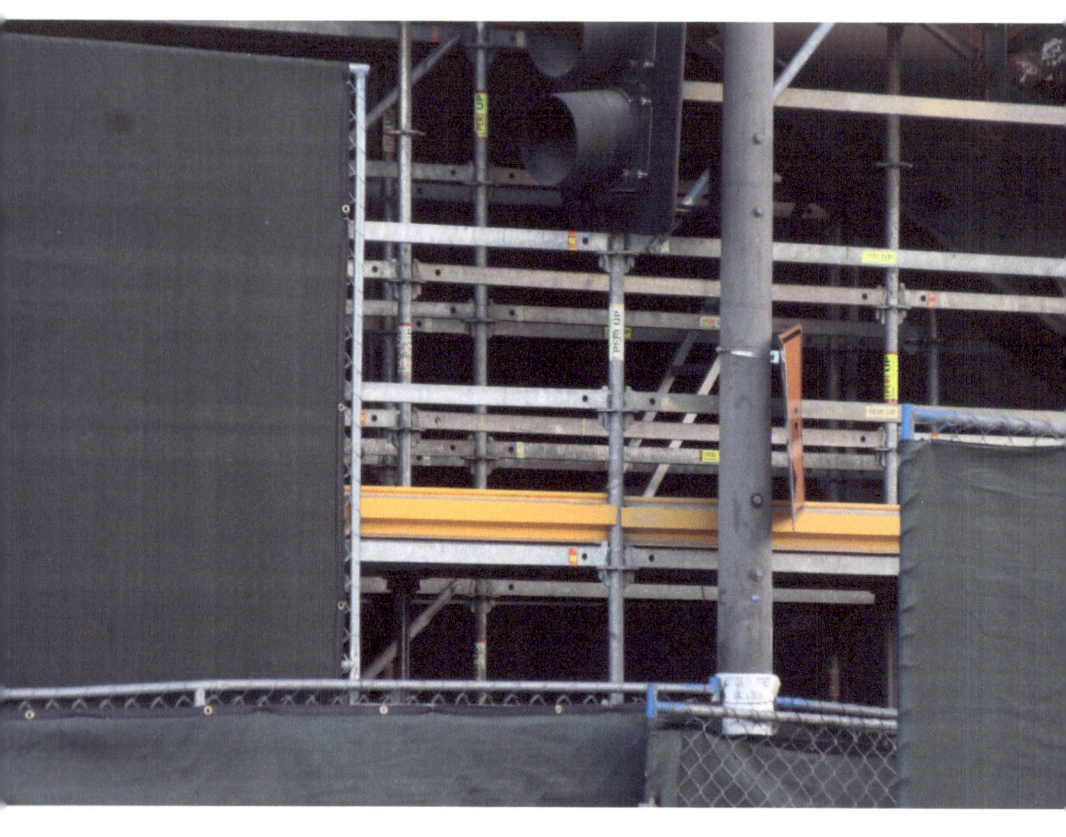

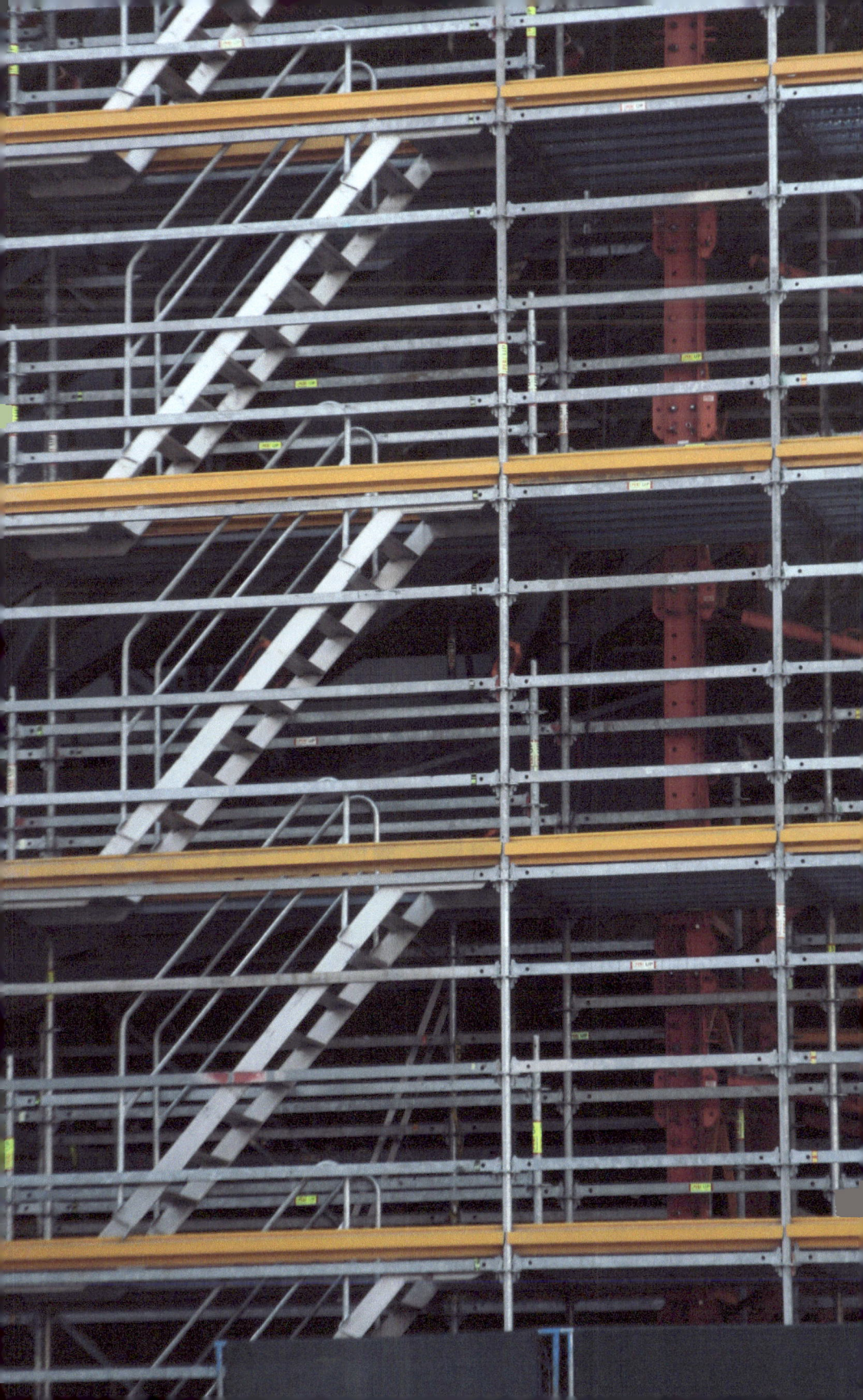

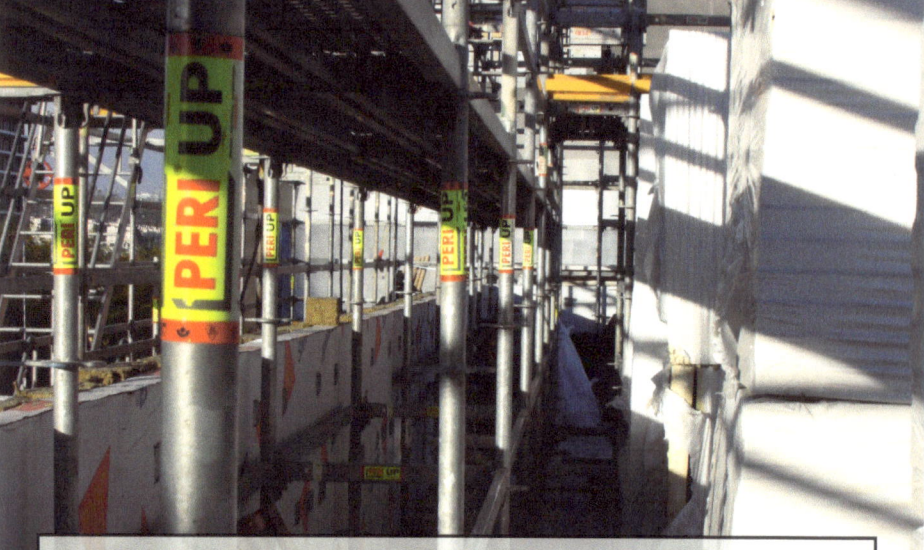

A Mark Dahle Portfolio

The New President

Terminal Three #4

This Mark Dahle Portfolio includes a colorful abstract painting, twenty-six beautiful photographs from Los Angeles, California, and a story about the new President of the Otto Party.

For ten days the news had contained reports of a large-scale radiation leak at Whitehorse and the information that the area was under quarantine. Nothing more. But it looked like tonight might be the night when details about MalPox – and perhaps the President – were released.

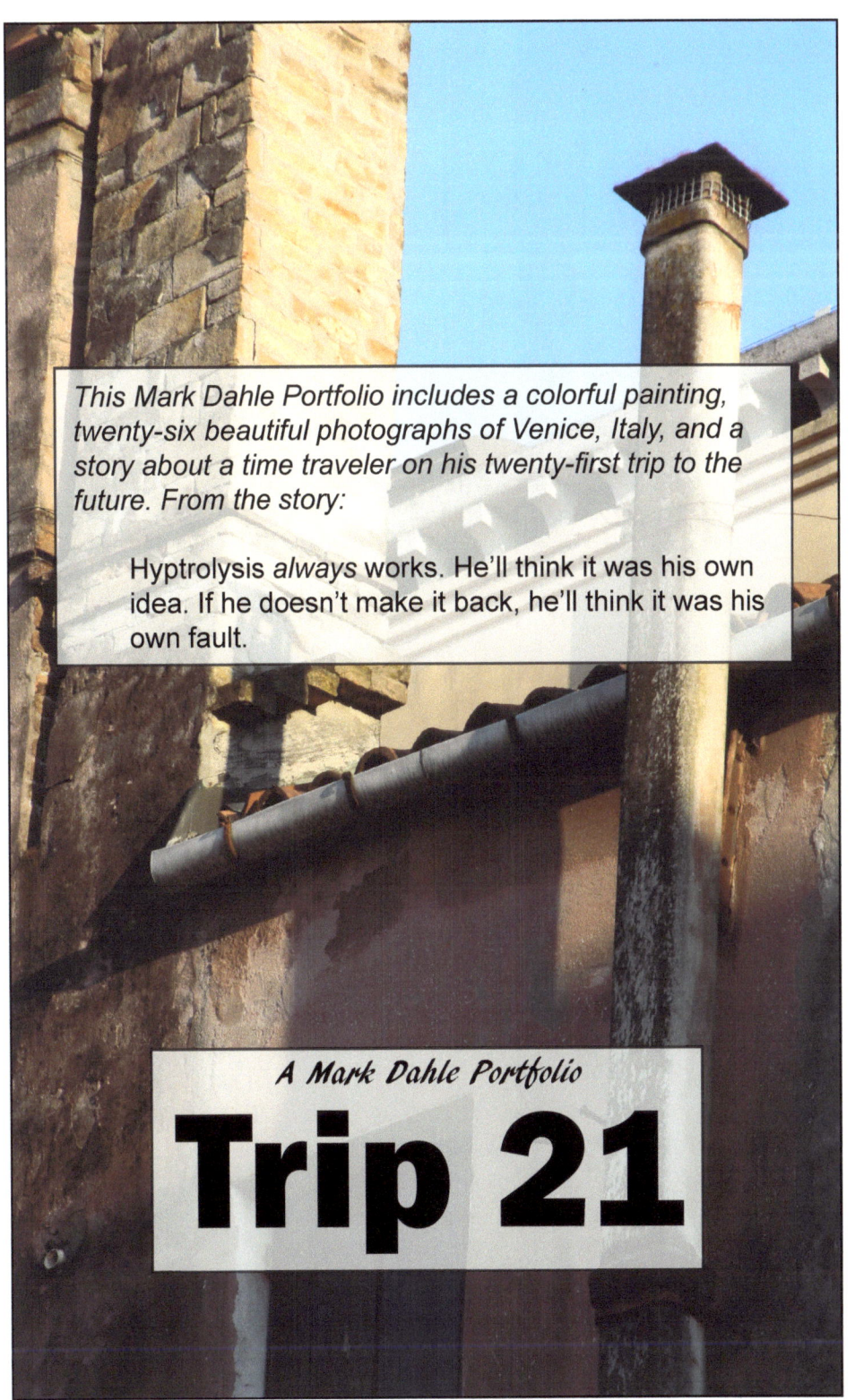

This Mark Dahle Portfolio includes a colorful painting, twenty-six beautiful photographs of Venice, Italy, and a story about a time traveler on his twenty-first trip to the future. From the story:

> Hyptrolysis *always* works. He'll think it was his own idea. If he doesn't make it back, he'll think it was his own fault.

A Mark Dahle Portfolio

Trip 21

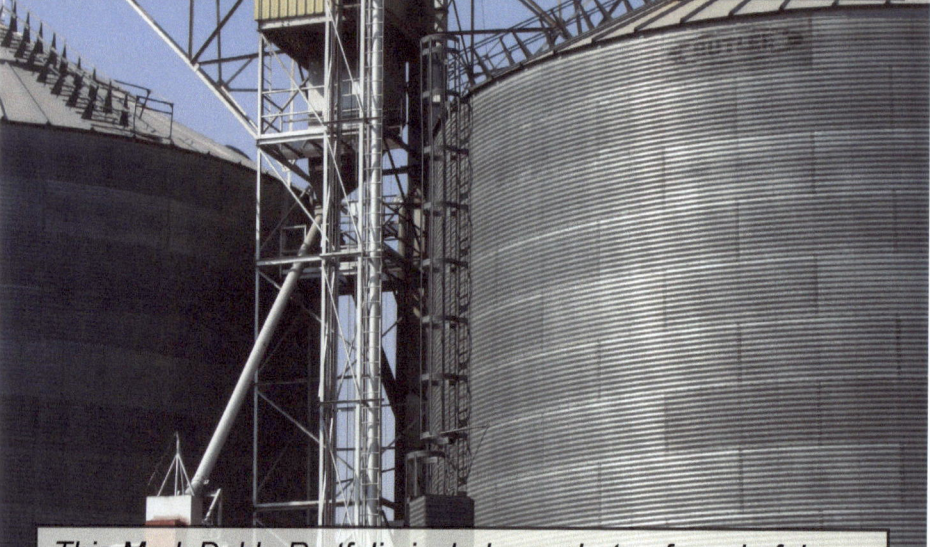

A Mark Dahle Portfolio

Monkey Brains
On Big River

Little Gibbon's Big Adventures #1

This Mark Dahle Portfolio includes a photo of a colorful abstract painting, twenty-six outstanding photographs from Spokane and Eastern Washington, and a story about a gibbon who liked adventures.

As he sailed down the river Monkey Brains could see his boot near the paddle he had forgotten on the dock. But he was going on an adventure, and he didn't care. Who needs a boot and a paddle when you want to have an adventure?

www.ingramcontent.com/pod-product-compliance
Lightning Source LLC
Chambersburg PA
CBHW040858180526
45159CB00001B/455